MYSTICISM and ECUMENISM

MYSTICISM
and ECUMENISM

by Robley Edward Whitson

SHEED AND WARD·NEW YORK

*Dedicated
to the
People and Worlds
of
Regina Laudis Monastery
and the
Sabbathday Lake Shaker Society
United in the Living Mysticism of Christ*

Contents

Introduction

Mysticism has been defined cynically as that which begins with mist and ends in schism. Unfortunately there are all too many historical examples of religious mysticism (at least so-called) that tend to confirm such an attitude. But the attitude itself, especially when it invades the thinking of the theologian, can betray a more serious question of orientation: How deeply is religious commitment realized? For, however we would define it and whatever norms of judgment we would devise to verify it, religious mysticism claims for itself an ultimacy in the individual's striving for a subjectively significant confrontation with God. The effectiveness of this claim, at least with regard to man's imagination, can be seen in the immediate interest the word mysticism evokes.

Yet this brings us to the first of many paradoxes to be encountered in a study of mysticism. In spite of the immediate interest mysticism as a subject arouses in even the most casual hearers or readers, extraordinary little systematic study has been made of the subject, whether from the point of view of theology, philosophy or scientific disciplines. And most of the work that has been undertaken has suffered from a consequent lack of interrelational and interdisciplinary background. This, in turn, often gives rise to one of two extremes: the reduction of mysticism to a very narrow and perhaps arbitrary area of phenomenology—at times attempting simply to explain it away; or the extension of mysticism to almost every category of human experience to the point of indefinability—arriving logically at near meaninglessness.

The purpose of the present work is to begin an investigation of religious mysticism as the confrontation of man and the Sacred. The scope of the investigation demands a study of materials drawn from various religious traditions, and approached in a variety of ways. It is appropriate, therefore, that this study be both theological and comparative. And since religious mysticism as actually encountered in mystics is integrally bound up with their religious commitments—indeed, would be meaningless without them—commitment itself must be involved in the study. Thus, it should be obvious that any study of this type must be basically introductory and exploratory, reaching out into a vast complex of unknowns heretofore barely touched, especially theologically.

If religious commitment must be involved in this type of study, then the commitment of the investigator must necessarily be identified and must be given an appropriate function within the structure of the work. Hence, it is required methodologically that an exploration of Christian mysticism be undertaken first, in terms of which a complementing comparative study of non-Christian traditions is possible. Since this second phase can reveal patterns of convergence (as well as of divergence), the comparative study inevitably will have bearing on the current theological dimension of ecumenism.

At the outset we must clarify the range of meaning proper to religious mysticism in this exploration. First, we intend to be concerned only with the mystical experience-complex within the context of religion as such. Without considering the possible mysticism in art, ideology or related areas, even if these areas are seen in a religious dimension, we are limiting our present interest to those *extraordinary experiences of confrontation of man with the Sacred* (however the Sacred may be conceived in any particular religious tradition). Thus, we will be dealing exclusively with mysticism as rooted in religious commitment.

The range is further narrowed by concentrating on what is properly the metaphysical dimension of religious mysticism. That is, our interest is directed exclusively toward mysticism as a process-experience of individuals apparently reflecting an ultimate relationship to the Sacred. Religious commitment orients the individual to Another, the Sacred; it is in this Other that he seeks fulfillment, it is this Other that gives him final significance. The ultimate theological dimension of religious mysticism, therefore, must be seen in terms of the metaphysical relationship of man to the Sacred insofar as the individual mystic is understandable subjectively only in terms of his commitment. Hence, the range of this study excludes direct consideration of psychological and other phenomena often (at least popularly) identified with mysticism. Also excluded for the same reason is consideration of psychological phenomena induced through hypnosis or drugs.* All such exclusion presumes nothing with regard to the authenticity or evaluation of "mystical phenomena." Rather, our orientation presumes that regardless of any external phenomena, the most fundamental dimension of religious mysticism is that which is immediately reflective of religious commitment and hence which establishes the significance of the human-Sacred relationship of unique and paramount importance to the mystic himself.

The types of materials available for this study impose their own methodological limitations. First, written materials as such can give evidence of the mystical (in the religious-metaphysical sense) insight of a writer or tradition of writers, but they are not

* Appendix II presents a series of extracts from *Psycho-Chemistry and the Religious Consciousness,* an article reporting preliminary findings and theory in this area.

themselves examples of mysticism as the subjective confrontation-state of the mystic. Hence, we must draw from a variety of types of writings which give us different insights into mysticism, and not merely from writings by mystics who are attempting direct expositions of their mystical experiences. For Christian mysticism it thus seems appropriate to draw from an area of Scripture which, though not a "mystical writing" as such, clearly reflects the meaning of Christian commitment, exhorts to the fulfillment of that commitment and is historically of maximum influence on the subjective formation of identifiable Christian mystics.

The selections from the writings of Christian mystics represent a wide range of thought, intention and presentation. There are many passages that are direct expositions of the mystic's interior experience, while other passages reveal his understanding of the commitment relationship expressed in Scriptural, theological, philosophical or poetic terms. Insofar as commitment relationship must be understood if we are to understand something of the expressions of mysticism, these widely diverse types of texts have been drawn together in complement to one another. The various passages selected from the writings of each mystic have been edited into single coherent texts with captional titles for the subdivision. Attention must be drawn to this procedure to acknowledge the effect in emphasis achieved through this editing, an effect that need not necessarily reflect the emphasis of the original writers. Our present interest is not in the analysis and evaluation of individual mystics, but in religious mysticism as reflected in given writers and traditions. Consequently, in searching for coherent and common structures embracing many individuals we are more interested in the presence of structural elements than in the relative emphasis placed upon such elements by this or that mystic. Hence, the editing of selections into single constructions is designed to give insight into the basic structure of the metaphysics of mysticism and not necessarily into the individuality of the mystic.

The comparison of non-Christian to Christian mysticism involves all of the above methodological factors as well as others entailed in comparative study as such. In spite of the vast resources of Judaic and Islamic mysticism,* these two traditions are not included in the comparative phase because of their close historical relation to Christianity. These three traditions share a common heritage in many theological, philosophical and cultural areas, and thus a comparison of Christian, Judaic and Islamic mysticism in the dimension of commitment relationship would not exhibit the degree of contrast which reveals the ecumenical dimension of religious mysticism. The traditions drawn from represent a wide spectrum of religious systems, extending back to pre-Christian antiquity and involving entitive theism, monism, apparent non-theism and humanism.

In attempting to select materials from these traditions, two problems must be faced: the cultural-linguistic barriers and the varieties of religious emphases. With regard to cultural-linguistic barriers, a decision must be made as to the procedure to be followed in presenting texts. For our present purposes we are concerned with comparing common structure rather than with an evaluation of differing emphases. Hence the texts have been simplified where necessary, eliminating elements whose proper exposition and understanding would necessitate considerable explanation. Such simplifications are always undesirable, can

---

* Judaic mysticism is well represented in the prophetic traditions of the Old Testament, especially in Isaiah, Ezekiel and Daniel; later Jewish mysticism has its most important embodiment in the Hasidic tradition. A tradition of Islamic mysticism arises some time after Mohammed and the formaton of the Qur'an, although Mohammed himself should be numbered among the mystics, and there are Qur'anic passages (see Appendix I) which serve as foundational elements of the later mysticism, the Sufist tradition, whose most famous mystic was Al-Ghazali, a contemporary of Bernard of Clairvaux.

xiv   *Introduction*

mislead dangerously and certainly distort the impression given
to the reader. Yet in the present instance they are an unfortunate
necessity. However they may distort the original particular elements and emphases, the simplifications employed here make
possible a broad comparison of structures which is valid within
the limits of an introductory exploration.

In facing the problems raised by the varieties of religious emphases when in the context of a comparison with Christianity,
we must recognize that a degree of simplification must be employed here as well, with a similar danger of distortion. Although
divisive areas are indicated, emphasis has been placed upon
similarities and possible lines of convergence. Caution must be
exercised, therefore, lest a superficial syncretism result. Obviously, the brief introduction to each selection of texts cannot be
exhaustive nor expressive of the elaboration and subtlety of each
tradition. Hence caution must be exercised again lest we reduce
the full impact of these complex and highly developed religious
traditions to the sparse outlines given here.

In preparing translations or versions of translations of the
texts chosen to represent each tradition, an attempt was made
to utilize sources that would be readily available to the reader.
Since many older works are being reissued (such as Legge's
translations of Eastern texts), it was thought advisable to draw
from these rather than from some more modern works. Where
required, modifications have been introduced. With regard to
completely new translations (such as in the case of all four
Christian writers), they have been kept as close as possible to
one or another of the standard or popular translations, again for
the reader's convenience.*

---

* The author wishes to express his gratitude to Sr. M. Paula Peck for research done in many of the areas of the textual materials used here, while
preparing a dissertation on the socio-cultural dimension of mysticism under the
author's mentorship ("The Cultural Expression of the Experience of Mystical
Union").

All of the above remarks indicate the bare outline of the many problems to be faced in this particular type of work. The choices of texts, interpretations, representatives of traditions, emphases and all the rest are all open to valid criticism on any number of specialized levels. All this notwithstanding, there is a real need for the exploration of mysticism in its theological dimension of confrontation, commitment and convergence. While admitting, therefore, the many limitations and unavoidable primitiveness of this present attempt, its claim of validity must rest upon the structures developed for the analytical systematics of a theology of mysticism.

-ONE-
Mysticism

The term *mysticism* is applied to a variety of human activities often possessing apparently little or nothing in common. On the level of social and political activity mysticism may be used to express the process of participation in and commitment to an ideological system. Thus in Marxism, for example, the ideology demands a total giving of self on the part of the individual—he must see himself as meaningless except within the collective mass, must seek all moral norms according to the sole criterion of the good of the collectivity, must attempt to submerge everything he is and has into a single, selfless mass consciousness. This may be spoken of as a form of mysticism in that it calls for a transcending of individuality in identity, action and awareness in favor of a kind of supreme reality towards which mankind is supposedly drawn.

The notion of mysticism is also applied to the area of artistic inspiration. It is made a part of the emotional involvement of the artist or it is the flood of emotion itself. Or if artistic inspiration is seen as an intuition then this is mysticism. We are faced with a situation calling for a penetration into the individual. Even with the externalization the artist produces—the sculpture, the painting, the poem—we cannot reach into the person. In the classic Western tradition the artist attempts to communicate something of his inspirational experience or insight to the beholder. The greater the artist the more effective is the communication, stirring the beholder to a recreation of the original experience. In the Oriental tradition the beholder is to be moved to a new creation individual to himself. Here the success of the artist is measured in terms of the number and depth of the new creations occasioned. Whichever tradition we view, the object is a type of intermediate communicating cause. It is not evidence of the experience itself and not simply an externalization of the emotion or intuition. We remain essentially in the realm of the personal, our appreciation of the process depending on some degree of involvement and insight.

Mysticism may be equated with a form of emotion identified by certain characteristics. Yet emotion is a response to *something*. This something is real insofar as the emotion is real. The emotion is a subjective reality but it can be in response to either a subjective or objective reality. In itself the emotional response does not betray which real is present. If we wish to study mysticism through emotion we must recognize that emotion is but part of the process.

The problem is narrowed when we consider the testimony of those who claim to have been involved in mysticism directly. We find that some clearly deny that it is an emotional experience. In some cases no emotion precedes the experience. In some cases emotion does not follow the experience. And over and over again witnesses maintain in the clearest of statements that at the heart of the experience there is a total absence of emotion, in fact there is nothing that can be related to what they have previously encountered.

Whether or not we eventually extend mysticism to embrace the widest possible range of experiences, our interest here is confined to religious mysticism. Therefore, we must discover if this highly subjective experience is capable of being structured, and must seek to frame a structural definition of mysticism.

Defining religion structurally as *the systematized interrelation of the human and the "suprahuman,"* religious mysticism necessarily involves the same subjects, the human and the suprahuman. As a system mysticism expresses a particular relationship between the subjects. The textual statements which will be analyzed from the different witnesses of the experience approach this relationship in terms of *union* or *oneness*. From the fact that the experiences as separated occurrences are not enduring, we must qualify this union or oneness as a *process*, as dynamic rather than static.

We can approach the testimony to the mystical process in two ways. The witnesses testify to a mystical experience. Here the emphasis is on the occurrence as personal and the witness speaks of an event in which he partook. The witnesses testify to a mystical state. Here the emphasis is on the process itself. As we shall find, each testimony reflects both approaches.*

THE MYSTICAL PROCESS

Defining structure as *an objective ordering of elements into a meaningful and significant totality* and applying it to religious mysticism, the mystical process assumes two aspects. Two elements, man and the Sacred Presence, are ordered into a totality, the mystical state. The system is the relationship of union, the actual (objective) ordering. The relationship of union is necessarily dynamic since it is *a coming into oneness* of the human and the Presence. The process is to be located in the dynamism

---

* For the classic works emphasizing the experiential in mysticism, cf. William James, *Varieties of Religious Experience,* and Evelyn Underhill, *Mysticism.* Important comparative studies of mysticism include: Dom Cuthbert Butler, *Western Mysticism;* F. S. C. Northrop, *The Meeting of East and West;* Joachim Wach, *Types of Religious Experience Christian and non-Christian;* R. C. Zaehner, *Mysticism Sacred and Profane.*

of the union, and since it relates two radically different subjects, the mystical process must embody two distinct aspects.

Man can approach the suprahuman rationally and relate himself to the Sacred through conceptualization. He can come into oneness by comprehension of the nature of the suprahuman insofar as such a nature can be conceived. We recognize that the comprehension of suprahuman nature is always inadequate since concept of the nature must be inadequate. Thus, we have the classic statement from the *Summa Theologiae* (Pt. 1, Q. 12, A. 2): ". . . The nature of God, however, cannot be seen by any created similitude representing the divine nature itself *as it really is.*" The inadequacy is an immediate consequence of the distinction made between the human and the transcendent suprahuman, however the latter is conceived. The Sacred is such precisely because it is totally *other.**

When we evaluate the content of proposed conceptualizations of the nature of the suprahuman, the very terms used betray the fact of inadequacy. *Transcendent* indicates that which goes beyond; *infinite* is a denial of boundaries or limitation; *eternal* negates time and temporal duration. All the concepts we form of the suprahuman are analogous. We choose characteristics proper to the human level and attempt to extend them positively to the suprahuman, recognizing that there is some similarity between the two levels but negating the limitations of the lower level. These concepts are valid within a given epistemological system, they do *reflect* reality, but they do not encompass the object, the Sacred. To express what the totally *other* is, we must accentuate differences. In other words, we know what we are, and the Other appears by contrast.

* For a treatment of this notion in terms of a psychological phenomenology, refer to the development of the "wholly other" in Rudolf Otto, *The Idea of the Holy.* This notion is taken into the context of Christian–non-Christian comparative mysticism in the same author's *Mysticism East and West.*

The mystical process of union, of coming into oneness, has a rational foundation in that it cannot be divorced from man's conceptualizations. On the rational level the mystics are seen to differ in their interpretation of the significance and religious orientation of the mystical state. Yet on what must be termed a non-rational level there is remarkable agreement found among mystics of widely varying religious traditions. There are two reasons at this point for speaking of a non-rational level. First, the impressive evidence of agreement in spite of diverse cultural and religious backgrounds should indicate that somehow conceptualization can be avoided in the mystical state. Second, mystics claim that in the mystical state they "know" the suprahuman precisely as Other and without concept.

One can admit the simple possibility of a mode of knowledge (for want of a better term) that is not conceptual, non-rational. One may be able to accept the testimony of mystics that there actually is such a mode. But an attempt to analyze the process of non-rational knowledge would seem to be patent absurdity. Obviously that which is non-conceptual does not exhibit a rational or conceptual structure. However, the non-rational mode is *reflected* in the *reactions* of the mystics. These reactions constitute the direct data of study and provide indirect access to the non-rational process itself.

The reactions to the mystical process are *signs* rather than concepts. It is true that on the surface they appear to be concepts, but further analysis reveals that the terms employed are designed to *affirm a fact*, the oneness with the Sacred Presence achieved in the mystical state, while avoiding direct statement of the *nature* of the Presence or of the union experienced. These signs stand in place of the Sacred as confronted and manifest the existential fact. The most impressive evidence for this interpretation is the number of terms each mystic employs in speaking of the state and the constant restatement of the experience—not to mention repeated and explicit denials of any attempt to conceptualize.

The mystical religious process, located in the dynamism of the union—the coming into oneness of the human and suprahuman—embodies two intellectual modes or aspects, the rational and the extra-rational. The process as rational has for one terminus a concept or concepts from which one moves through a process of *rational knowledge* to a comprehension of the other terminus, resulting in a judgment of the essence of the suprahuman. The process as extra-rational has for one terminus a sign or signs from which one moves through a process of *extra-rational realization* to an apprehension of the other terminus, resulting in the existential Presence of the suprahuman. This rational/extra-rational process can be represented by the following diagrammatic formula:

I. *Rational*:

concept————————→comprehension: judgment
(knowledge)   (essence)

II. *Extra-rational*:

sign————————→apprehension: Presence
(realization)   (existence)

According to this schematization the rational mode of the process begins with an intellectual idea, the *concept*, which is inadequate because of its object. The process leads through *knowledge* of the concept to a *comprehension* of its object. (Note that we are unconcerned here with the formulation of a particular theory of knowledge.) The comprehension is also inadequate since it depends on an inadequate concept. The comprehension involves ideas of attributes of the suprahuman Presence and hence issues in a *judgment* concerning the suprahuman essence or nature. The rational mode of process is found in the mystical texts when they deal with conceptualizations of the nature, limitations and attributes of the suprahuman.

The extra-rational mode of the process begins with a *sign*. This is a symbol of the object as a reality, a present fact, and need not reflect the nature of the object. The sign can be any element suitable as a manifestation and need not indicate a properly rational connection with the object it represents. The process leads through *realization* of the sign to an *apprehension* of the object. The realization is a deep awareness and confrontation of the existence of the *Presence*. The apprehension involves a union or oneness achieved in the awareness of the Presence.

The realization or awareness is the key to the contrast between the rational and extra-rational modes of process. The difference between realization and knowledge can be seen in a common human experience outside the mystical state, the love of one human person for another. Whether this love is found in a parental-filial relationship, between spouses or between friends, the act of love itself escapes definition in concepts. It is impossible for one to *prove* rationally that he loves. He cannot explain *why* he loves this particular person although he can recognize characteristics that attract. Beyond the emotional level, human love reaches into the ultimate self-identity of the object which, as totally unique—"totally other"—cannot be conceptualized. In its deepest significance love is a state of oneness or union with another, the confrontational apprehension of the object as a present reality. There is an obvious parallel indicated here between the relationship of human love and the oneness with the Presence proposed in the mystical state. This is reflected clearly in the writings of most mystics who see mystical union as love and express it through symbols of marriage and filiation. For them human love and mystical union differ not in the extra-rational process but in the objects achieved, human or suprahuman.

In all of these considerations we are supposing a distinction between the fulfillment of the mystical process and the emotions. If emotion is a response to a stimulus and not something independent in itself, the distinction is valid and necessary. The mystics claim that the stimulus is the union with a real suprahuman. But in accepting the distinction between emotion and mystical state we simply accept the integral independence of the mystical state as proposed.

Both the rational and extra-rational mode of process as expressed in the two formularies can be reversed. In the case of the process as rational, comprehension can lead to concept (a whole analyzed and reduced to its component parts). In the process as extra-rational, the experience of Presence can lead to the choice of a sign to express it. Both these reversals are to be found in the mystical state, and they correlate mysticism with the proposed activity of prophets in the role they claim as intermediaries of the revelation of Divinity. (Note that prophets as thought of here are not predictors of the future but witnesses of the Sacred, as exemplified classically in the Hebrew tradition.)

A warning is necessary concerning the distinction we are making between comprehension and apprehension as well as the schematization of the rational and extra-rational. As presented, comprehension and apprehension seem clearly distinguishable, but in practice this may not be the case. The difficulty arises from the limitations that language imposes on the mystics. When the mystics use concepts these must be framed in analogous terms since the object cannot be encompassed in human language. It is therefore difficult at times to determine whether concept or sign is being used. This problem can be overcome, however, by a comparison of a wide range of texts. With regard to the schematization, it must be remembered that this is a formulation to make analysis of diverse expressions possible, not the proposal of a theory of knoweldge as rational-intuitive or the like.

THE MYSTICAL STATE

Having discussed the basis of religious mysticism with a formulation of the rational and extra-rational process as the relation of the human and suprahuman, we arrive at the last essential theoretical consideration, the analysis of the mystical state itself. Following the structural definition of religious mysticism as a process of union between the human and Presence, the analysis of the state achieved through the process is to be made according to structure. This procedure is designed to allow the various mystical writers to define their own experience of the state in appropriated phenomenological terms. A comparative study of the structure exhibited should then demonstrate the common elements present between systems of mysticism. A further comparison of the mysticism of differing religious systems should reveal the basis for such differences that appear among mystical traditions. Thus, ultimately, we hope to lay the foundation for an inter-system of the mystical state, ecumenically involving the religious systems themselves and the testimonies of individual adherents.

The structure of the mystical state entails three fundamental categories: the agents of the union, the dynamics of oneness and the essential characteristics of the act. As required in the exteriorization of the subjective state and in the nature of the data as elements in a verbal manifestation, all three categories necessarily reflect *directly* only the participation of the human subject. The suprahuman is reflected *indirectly*, but, as we should expect, the expression is confined within the limits of the religious system to which the mystic is committed.

The structure of the mystical state may be formulated as follows:

I. Agents of the Union
    A. Human subject—a conscious agent
    B. Suprahuman object—Presence, the Sacred
        1. transcendence of the object
        2. other attributes of the object
II. Dynamics of Oneness
    A. To be one with another (union)
    B. To be one *in se* (fusion, absorption, identification)
III. Essential Characteristics of the Human Act
    A. Donational—giving of self
    B. Voluntary—a union of will
        1. active
        2. passive
        3. both active and passive
    C. Purposeful—freely desired rather than accidental
    D. Durational—the mystical event as related to other events in time
        1. permanent (relatively)
        2. transient
    E. Particularized—union with a specific object only
    F. Exclusive—requiring abandonment of other desires
    G. Personal—direct experience of object by subject
(Note: one characteristic normally considered essential to an act of union as love, mutuality, is omitted since only

aspects pertaining to the human participation in union can appear as elements of structure.)

What heretofore have been referred to as the subjects of the relationship, the human and suprahuman, are now distinguished as subject and object to reflect the strictly human orientation of the evidence of the mystical state. The suprahuman is identified directly only as Presence. The transcendence of the Presence is necessarily an attribute common to non-monistic* mysticism, while other attributes (or at least the choice of such attributes) are postulated within the bounds of the religious system of the mystic.

The notion of oneness as being one with another in a form of union suggests the basis for the consistent use of the term *love* by the mystics. This should suggest further the basis for the emotional content so often characteristic of the mystical experience. Whatever the exact process may be whereby the emotional patterns of mysticism are stimulated, it appears that we must see it as somehow parallel to the condition of human love. In the analysis of the data the expression of divine love is reduced to this category in the sense of union defined as being one with another.

In the essential characteristics of the act of union only evidence reflecting the subject is considered. When the mystic speaks of characteristics of the Presence, this must represent evidence of his evaluation of attributes of the suprahuman object. By treating this latter evidence under the first category of the structure, it is possible to analyze the act of union as

---

* A monistic religious system presumes that there is only one actual entity in existence, the Divinity—all other entities are either pure illusions and hence not entities at all (so in Hinduism, the Godhead *Brahman* alone exists, all else is pure illusion), or the entities are divine emanations and hence are actually parts or aspects of the Godhead (as in various forms of pantheism).

independent from the particulars of the religious system to which the mystic is committed. In characterizing the act as personal no reference is made to the Presence as a person. Only the personality of the human subject is proposed.

In speaking of the mystical state instead of the mystical experience, we are implying a distinction as was briefly noted previously. The distinction does not indicate a distinction in kinds of mysticism—intuitive rather than emotional, for example. We are attempting to distinguish an emphasis, on our part and also on the part of mystical writers.

From our point of view we find it difficult to locate any objective basis for judging another's experience unless we have gone through the experience ourselves. Even then it seems that we must compare experiences as subjective participations. Disciplines such as psychology attempt to reduce experiences to common patterns, and a certain objectivity can be attained. But the very notion of an experience seems to exclude full communicability. In the case of a mystical experience with the mystic proclaiming his total inability to communicate, objectivity appears absolutely impossible.

-TWO-
Christian Mystics

The four mystics chosen to represent the Christian tradition in mysticism are separated from one another by periods of roughly five centuries. Each is typical of an era. The author of the First Johannine Letter portrays the thinking of the formative Apostolic period of Christianity as it emerges into the Graeco-Roman world from its Judaic beginnings. Augustine stands more or less at the close of the Roman era during which the Christian community had reached social stability, practical dominance of the Mediterranean peoples and an intellectual fusion with the Greek philosophical tradition. Bernard of Clairvaux comes at a period marked by the consolidation of the new Christian civilization of the Middle Ages. It is the beginning of an era of confrontation and interchange with the East, expecially with Islam which reaches the full development of its own Sufist mystical tradition in the person of Abu Hamid al Ghazali, a contemporary of Bernard. John of the Cross, the last representative we shall consider, writes at the time of the dissolution of the united Christendom of Western Europe. It is the period of reform, the Protestants attempting to return to the way of life of the primitive period, Catholics like John of the Cross seeking to reform the Church in its cumulative historical development.

There are countless mystics accepted by Christians and the selection of these four is designed only to concentrate on representatives of the tradition who exemplify the historical process of development correlated with changing cultural emphases.

THE WRITERS

The Johannine Author. Traditionally the Apostle John is held to be the author of the fourth gospel, three epistles and the Apocalypse of the Christian Scriptures. There has been considerable dispute among scholars since the nineteenth century on this point, with attribution of these works or parts of them to John the Elder, John of Jerusalem, John the Younger or John the Seer. Whatever position one wishes to take on the matter,* it is sufficient for us to note that all these documents reflect a single general tradition. We might be content to speak of a Johannine School representing several authors and editors of the apostolic period as the source of the documents. As regards mysticism, all the documents of this group reflect a fairly well-defined interest centered on the New Covenant commandment of love. The dating of the texts is placed at the close of the first and beginning of the second centuries. If one holds to a single author, John the Evangelist, the date given traditionally for his death is 110 A.D.

We are taking the First Johannine Letter as representative of the apostolic mystical tradition,† and the version used here is a

---

* A useful summary of the current thinking on the authorship question is given in Neil Alexander, *The Epistles of John* (New York: The Macmillan Company, 1962), pp. 23–27.

† However, the First Letter was not written as a mystical treatise, but as a magisterial pastoral letter to guide certain of the early Christian communities in the recognition and rejection of gnostic and related theological errors. Like other New Testament letters, it is occasioned by practical problems. But its approach to the current issues entails the mystical dimension of Christianity, and later Christians will draw from it in this light. (For a summary of the theological crisis occasioning the Letter, cf. reference to N. Alexander, *op. cit.*)

translation from the Greek text arranged into lines reflecting thought patterns in the original Greek, and divided into sections with interpretive headings.

Augustine of Hippo. Augustine (354–430 A.D.), Bishop of Hippo in North Africa, and Doctor and Father of the Church, represents a combination of philosopher and theologian. The works cited here cover the period from 386 to 427 and represent a wide range of material, theological, philosophical, exegetical and autobiographical (The *Confessions*). There is a notable contrast between the passages from Augustine and those from the Johannine Letter. Augustine's works are highly systematized, reflecting the development of formal theology in the three centuries following the composition of the original Scriptures. The theological development, in turn, involves the adaptation of philosophical method and conceptualizations which necessarily determine much of the approach and emphasis in Augustine's treatment of doctrine.

Bernard of Clairvaux. It may be said that Bernard was the greatest Christian figure of the twelfth century. In his lifetime (1090–1153 A.D.) he was responsible for a major reform in western monasticism, was deeply involved in the complex social and political movements of two generations and became a widely reputed teacher of various aspects of spirituality, including that of the mystical state. The texts drawn from his many writings deal directly with mysticism. He is far less influenced by a formal philosophical treatment of the subject than was Augustine, and shows the attempt to communicate meaningfully concerning his mystical experience by means of metaphor and symbol rather than by conceptualization. Most of the material used here is drawn from treatises on the spiritual life written for his monks and from an extensive series of sermons (The *Sermones in Cantica Canticorum*) written towards the end of his life. The dual aspect of his life as contemplative and active leader in the affairs of Christendom enables us to see Christian mysticism in a considerably different perspective from that of the scriptural or philosophical traditions exemplified in the Johannine and Augustinian texts.

John of the Cross. Juan de la Cruz (1542–1591) is usually accepted as the greatest theologian of Christian mysticism in meeting the problem of providing a systematic description of the mystical state and experience. He writes at a difficult time, the height of the Catholic-Protestant conflict.* Considering the subject matter of his works it is not surprising that some of his over-careful Catholic contemporaries viewed the writings and his participation in the internal reform of the Church with serious suspicion. The *Spiritual Canticle* and the *Living Flame of Love*, both mystical treatises, were written in prison and later revised. The second redaction is used here since it would represent the mature intention of the author. Material from the *Ascent of Mount Carmel* and the *Dark Night of the Soul*, which are principally ascetical works, is also used where it pertains to mysticism. The presentation of mysticism by John of the Cross provides us with notable contrasts to the other three writers, especially in the area of the integration of doctrinal commitment with his systematization of the mystical state.

Following the plan devised in presenting the text of the First Johannine Letter, the variety of statements drawn from the writings of Augustine, Bernard and John of the Cross have been translated and arranged into lines reflecting thought patterns in the original languages, and interpretive headings have been introduced to draw the otherwise diverse texts together. Thus, in

---

* In the present study we have avoided the entire area of post-Reformation Catholic and Protestant mysticism because of the extraordinary complexity of the theological and hence interpretive problems involved. It should be obvious, however, that this area is of great potential value in developing inter-Christian ecumenism.

effect, something approaching a single document emerges to represent the thought of each writer, the form closely approximating that of the Johannine Letter. Obviously, the selection of passages, their internal division into the lines and the correlating sequence with its titles constitute an interpretation of the thought of the original authors. It is to be hoped that this interpretation is not far from their own minds.

In the Christian experience of the mystical state the Presence involved in the act of union as its object and terminus is identified unquestionably as God. The Christian's estimation of mysticism as a dynamic process is thus inseparable from the notion of Divinity. Accordingly we must relate the materials we investigate under the aspects of agents, dynamics and characteristics to the rational and extra-rational modes of the mystical process expressed by the Christian mystics in terms of Deity. The experience as an approach to God is analyzed as

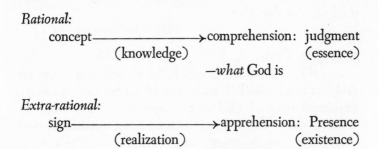

Rational:
concept ─────────────→ comprehension: judgment
        (knowledge)   (essence)
              ─*what* God is

Extra-rational:
sign ─────────────→ apprehension: Presence
        (realization)   (existence)
              ─*that* God is

Augustine, Bernard and John of the Cross make specific statements concerning these concepts in the following four passages.

Augustine:
What then, brethren, shall we say of God? For if you have been able to comprehend what you would say, then it

is not God. If you have been able to comprehend it, then you have comprehended something else instead of God. If you have been able to comprehend Him as you think, by so thinking you have deceived yourself. This then is not God, if you have comprehended it. But if it be God, then you have not comprehended it. Therefore how would you speak of that which you cannot comprehend?

(Sermons on Selected Lessons
of the New Testament, 52:16)

Bernard of Clairvaux:
. . . also I would willingly define contemplation as a clear and certain intuition of things by the eye of the spirit, or, in other words, an act by which the spirit grasps a known indubitable truth. As for meditation, I would say that it is an effort of the mind, an application of the spirit in seeking the truth. Nevertheless, the words are often used one for the other.

(De Consideratione, 2:5)

John of the Cross:
. . . there is something which, I feel, still remains to be said, a matter which I know has yet to be said—a clearly imprinted trace of God that is revealed to the soul and which it must follow; a most exalted understanding of God that cannot be expressed, and for that reason is termed "something"; and if the other thing that I understand inflicts upon me the wound and sore of love, this that I cannot entirely understand, but feel most deeply, slays me.

(Spiritual Canticle, 7:9)

. . . the soul approaches God more closely by not understanding than by understanding . . . God cannot be apprehended by the soul.

(Living Flame of Love, 3:48)

In reference to the statement of John of the Cross that God cannot be apprehended, it is clear from the context that the writer does not give the meaning we are using for the term *apprehension*. While we contrast apprehension with comprehension, it is evident that if "the soul approaches God more closely by not understanding than by understanding," apprehension and comprehension must be interchangeable terms for the author. If such were not the case and John of the Cross intended to use the term in the sense employed by us, he would be denying the very experience he attempts to expose in two treatises.

The process described by the Christian mystics is not rational. Concepts are not present in the mystical act. A sign stands at the beginning of the process, but it does not *represent* God to the consciousness of the mystic. The sign simply *designates* the fact of presence. The sign has no intellectual content to be grasped or understood. The sign points to Reality, occasions the beginning of a realization of or awakening to Something *confronting* the subject. We might say that the sign is the threshold beyond which is a totally different realm of consciousness: it is the end of self-consciousness and the beginning of selfless-consciousness. The mystic moves on from the sign and immediately apprehends the existence of the transcendent Presence. Bernard tries to delineate this crucial moment:

No doubt you ask how I am able to recognize that He is present, since His ways are incomprehensible. But He is alive and efficacious, and as soon as He comes to me He awakens my sleeping soul. He stirs, enervates and wounds my heart which had been like a stone and was sick. He comes also to root up, to destroy, to build, to plant, to water that which was dry, to enlighten that which was in shadows, to loosen that which was bound, to enflame that which was cold, to straighten that which was crooked, and

to smoothe that which was rough and twisted, so that my
soul may bless the Lord and all that is in me may bless
His Holy Name. It is thus that the Word, the Spouse, in
coming within me sometimes does not make known His en-
tering by any mark, neither by His voice nor by His face
nor by His step. In the end, I do not know Him by any
movement on His part; I do not perceive by any of my
senses that He has slipped into the depths of my soul. I
recognize His presence only by the movement of my heart
as I have said; I note the power of His virtue by the flight
of vices and by the abatement of passions which it effects
in me.

(Sermons on the Canticle of Canticles, 74:6)

As described in this passage we have an exposition of the process that fits our analysis of the extra-rational mode very closely.
The text also brings out the notion of the process being reversed,
that is, instead of moving from sign to Presence, there can be a
movement from Presence to sign. In both cases it is clear that there
is a link between rational and extra-rational consciousness through
the sign—the *mark* of Bernard which may precede the entrance.

CHRISTIAN MYSTICISM

From the cumulative effect of the text from all four Christian
writers, we shall discover that they are in agreement on several
key points.

First, the Presence—God—can never be comprehended, because of transcendence. Therefore, realization of God as proposed in the mystic's evaluation of the mystical state cannot be
rational. Concepts cannot be the means to comprehend God from
the very fact that He is totally Other. The absolute distinction
made between man and this *otherness* results in the impossibility

of representing directly the Other within the conceptual range
of the intellect. Concepts represent God indirectly as reflected in
the effects, the creatures, which He causes.* The full realization
of God by the mystic is therefore the result of an extra-rational
process.

The mystics agree on another closely related point. Granted
that the experience of the mystical state is not intellectual in the
sense of conceptual, nonetheless the extra-rational level is not
completely unrelated to the rational. Intellectual elements appear
in an anterior anticipation of the mystical state and also in a
posterior reflection on it whereby the mystic attempts to relate
his selfless-consciousness to self-consciousness. Like any man the
mystic is an integrated entity and cannot tolerate dismember-
ment. If he could not find meaning for the mystical act—necessarily intellectual, conceptual meaning—the mystical process
would be one of annihilation as far as the Christian would be
concerned. The Christian, then, relates the sign of the extra-
rational process to conceptual knowledge, and analyzes the *effect*
the experience of Presence has had on him interiorly. The result
is at least a knowledge of contrasts. From this the mystic grasps
something of the significance the mystical act should have for
his total existence. In this he integrates the experience with his
religious tradition. It should be noted that it is his *experience*
that is referred to the religious tradition and not the mystical
state itself. In the state he confronts Presence existentially, without concept, without consciousness of self. Upon analysis of his
experience he *knows* it is God. The signs of the process, bridg-
ing the gulf between the rational and extra-rational, relate the

* ". . . since every agent reproduces itself insofar as it is an agent, and
everything acts according to the manner of its form, the effect must resemble
the form of the agent in some way. . . . In this way all created things, insofar
as they are beings, resemble God as the first and universal principle of all
beings." (*Summa Theologiae:* Pt. 1, Q. 4, A. 3)

Presence experienced to the Christian's intellectual experience of God emerging from reason and Faith. We can locate the peculiarly Christian characteristics of mystics we have been studying in the rational mode of the process and, often enough, in the signs by which they designate beginnings of the extra-rational mode.

Finally, the Christian mystics reflect three aspects of the interrelation of the rational and extra-rational pertaining to religious system or tradition:

1. The significance of the experience is determined in accordance with concepts arising from other areas of the mystic's knowledge, principally speculative knowledge from philosophy and theology.

2. The beliefs of the religious tradition establish or condition a movement toward seeking the experience.

3. These beliefs also provide a framework to make the consciousness of the experience intelligible.

The Christian maintains that man's end entails a divinizing union with the Godhead through incorporation into Christ. Therefore, the significance of the mystical experience is seen in terms of a foretaste of this enduring union of eternity. It is also a means of drawing certain persons to a higher participation in spiritual leadership of the faithful. The whole concept of incorporation into Christ, beginning with the acceptance of the gift of Faith and continuing through frequent mystical contact with Christ in the sacraments, certainly conditions Christians—at least some—to seek the presence of Christ contemplatively. In the practice of the Christian Church from the beginning there has been constant encouragement given to *every* Christian to pursue meditative prayer. Contemplation, the ideal result of meditation, is definitely regarded as within the realm of mysticism. The regard in which the Church holds contemplative mysticism can be seen in the traditional institutions in which the formal contemplative life is embodied, the anchoritic and cenobitic religious orders. The Christian religious tradition places the mystical experience in a setting in which the individual and his activities are always found in a social dimension. Thus, the individual can achieve salvation and ultimate divinization only through unity with the Divine-Human Christ, and since all who are divinized are similarly united to Christ, all are united to each other. Hence, the acts of one man incorporated into the *Mystical Body* of Christ have meaning beyond the level of the individual. Seen within this setting, therefore, the Christian's mystical experience will have a far different meaning for him than the possible mystical experience of an isolated individualist who regards man as ultimately non-social.

The role of the sign in the extra-rational process has been discussed in reference to its function as a nexus between the self-conscious and selfless-conscious states experienced by the Christian mystic, and we have noted that this role can be the basis for identifying a common factor between particular mystical systems. The sign is also a principal factor in determining that a report of the mystical experience belongs to a specified mystical system. In spite of the fact that the sign designates the fact of Presence rather than represents its nature, the sign nevertheless has relevance to the object it designates, at least in the mind of the mystic—otherwise it would not be employed. The sign, then, means something in the rational order, and by virtue of this meaning it is a fitting designation of the Something in the extra-rational order. The sign is ambivalent as a relating mechanism between the two orders, having meaning in one but not in the other. The effect that the choice of signs has in determining the specification of distinct mystical traditions or systems can be seen by reviewing the most important signs used by the four Christian mystics in the texts gathered here. There are over fifty major signs which seem to fall into three general categories: theological signs (closely but not necessarily exclusively associated with doctrinal and scriptural tradition), philosophical signs (pertaining primarily to attributes that can be postulated from reason), and accommodational signs (adaptations of metaphors, imagery, etc.).

1. *Theological signs:*
    Lord God, Father.
    Word, Son, Jesus, Christ, Bridegroom, Incarnation, Bread.
    Holy Spirit, Fountain.
    Light, Life, Love.
2. *Philosophical signs:*
    All-Ruler, Most High, Majesty, Lord of the universe, Lord of eternity, God of ages.
    Creator, Cause, Supreme Principle, Supreme Author, Supreme Beatitude.
    Being of God, divine nature, divine will, divine Spirit, Truth, Spirit of Truth.
    Intelligible light, inaccessible light, incorruptible, inviolate, immutable, Omnipotent.
    Power, Wisdom, Glory, Peace, Serenity, Good.
    Person, One, Reality, That Which Is.
3. *Accommodational signs:*
    Face, mouth, feet, hand.
    Touch, kiss, marriage, Beloved, Spouse.
    Sweetness, beauty, infusion, living flame, abyss of splendors.

The great majority of the signs undeniably reveal a Christian context, and all but a few show adherence to belief in a personal divinity. Many of the signs of the philosophical category do have a particular theological relevance within the Christian religious tradition, but they have been placed in a more neutral category since we find these signs used in non-Christian traditions.

Grouping the principal signs together should bring out forcefully the key role the sign plays in the mystical process. On the one hand it is obvious that the sign ties the mystical experience into the religious system of the mystic. On the other hand the variety of the signs should demonstrate their relativity, that is, the fact that they can be interchanged without altering the significance of the extra-rational mode of the process. Thus, we shall find that the sign is a basis for establishing both the common ground and the specific differences between mystical systems.

One final point remains to be settled concerning Christian mysticism: the place officially accorded mysticism in the doctrinal structure. We have already noted that mysticism is institutionalized and given a social dimension, but we must determine the place the mystical system occupied in doctrine. In the Third Book of the *Summa Contra Gentiles* Thomas Aquinas gives us the classic statements on the question.

1. The end of intellectual beings:

. . . God is the end of each being, and thus, as far as it is possible to it, each being intends to be united to God as its last end. Now a being is more closely united to God *by reaching in some way to the very substance of God*, which happens when it knows something of the divine substance. . . . Therefore the intellectual substance tends to the knowledge of God as its last end. (Chapter 25)

2. Ultimate happiness in contemplation:

Now it is impossible that man's ultimate happiness should consist in contemplation based on the understanding of first principles, for this is most imperfect as it is most universal, containing potentially the knowledge of things. Moreover, it is the beginning and not the end of human inquiry, and comes to us from nature and not through the pursuit of truth. Nor does it consist in contemplation based on the sciences which have the lowest things for their object, because happiness must consist in an operation of the intellect regarding the most noble of intelligible objects. It follows then that *man's ultimate happiness consists in wisdom* founded on the consideration of divine things. (Chapter 37)

3. Seeing God in His essence:

We may take it as a sign of this that the more the mind is raised to the contemplation of spiritual things, the more it is withdrawn from sensible things (i.e., things of the senses). Now the divine substance is the ultimate term to which contemplation can reach, and thus the mind that sees the divine substance must be wholly freed from the corporeal senses, *either* by death *or* by rapture. Therefore, it is said attributed to God (Exodus 33:20): Man shall not see me and live. (Chapter 47)

. . . the divine substance cannot be seen by the intellect by means of any created species (i.e., conceptually). Therefore, if God's essence is to be seen at all, it must be that the intellect sees it through the divine essence itself. So in that vision the divine essence is both the object and the medium of vision. . . .

This *immediate vision of God* is promised to us in Sacred Scripture (I Corinthians 13:12): We see now through a glass in an obscure manner, but then (it will be) face to face. . . . (Chapter 51)

. . . those things which serve for the perfection of intellectual vision are called light . . . the disposition whereby
the created intellect is raised to the intellectual vision of the
divine substance is correctly called the light of glory . . .
since in God *to be* is the same as to *understand,* and since
to all He is the cause of their understanding, He is said to
be the light. . . . (Chapter 53)

Contemplation of God, vision of the Light through the light
of glory, is the only end of man for the Catholic tradition of
Christianity. The mysteries of Faith and the Sacraments, the
incorporation into Christ in His Mystical Body, all lead to the
unity of Love, perfect at death but arising also here and now
in mystic rapture.

THREE

The Christian Writings

FIRST JOHANNINE LETTER

The First Letter of St. John is a unique monument of the Apostolic Faith as preserved within the body of the Scriptures. Unlike the Gospels, it speaks exclusively of one theme: Jesus, the God of Love. Yet in spite of its singular beauty and clarity, the Letter is one of the most neglected documents of the New Testament. Perhaps this is to be accounted for in part by the very simplicity of its theme and style, our imaginations being more attracted to the wealth and variety of detail to be found in the other writings. Quite possibly the recognition of this attraction should give us pause: Are we reading the Scriptures to gratify a curiosity about Christ rather than to seek to see Christ as did the Apostles?

Certainly it is most desirable to know the details of the Apostolic teachings which lay down the great lines of our understanding of the Christian message. But is the purpose of that message information? Or rather should we seek Christ Himself as encountered by the Apostles—the Divine-Human Being, the Ultimate Reality, the Source of our Existence? Our understanding of the teachings preserved by the Church in her first writings is a means to an end, not the end itself. The Christian message, the good news, is not a formula of words. It is the proclamation of the Word, the Divinity who has revealed Himself once and for all incarnate as Jesus. The words we read lead us to realize

37

that infinite Word who is beyond our understanding, who is incomprehensible, who simply is.

This letter of St. John does not tell us about Christ, it identifies Him: He is God. This, for St. John, is the Christian Faith, the acceptance of the self-revelation of God in Jesus. God has revealed Himself in countless ways to countless people: moving them to realize His presence through the understanding that He is the Creator of all, drawing them by the interior communication of Himself to seek Him in the life of dedication, and inspiring them through the realization of His Will to unify themselves with Him in the spirit. But beyond this, God has appeared to us absolutely in His Incarnation in such a way that we are able to approach Him as one of us.

In the last analysis, this is all there is to Christianity: Christ. But this all is the limitless All who embraces everything that is.

He has appeared finally in the latter days. After millennia of seeking, man suddenly came face to face with his origin and destiny revealed in Christ. Jesus is conceived and born into the world. He lives the archetypal life of the new mankind. He passes through the terrifying transformation of life into death into new life. In glory from the tomb He shows Himself to the Apostolic Church. They do not see simply a triumphant humanity, but the Theophany, the Godhead revealed.

This realization of the total Christ is the Faith of the Church, given through the Apostles alone. This Faith has not come to destroy the realization achieved by men in their search of God. It fulfills them—all of them—by drawing all truth together in the living Truth of the Word.

Yet to man is left the continuing task of realization. To each age and people the Revealed Christ is made known by the Church, witnessing the Faith of the Apostles. First to Israel, then to Greece and Rome and the nations that rose from them. Now, in our time, to the Africa emerging into history and to the venerable lands of the East clothed in ancient wisdom. Each brings to Christianity its unique achievement, however it may be expressed: the truths born of the search for God. And to each Christianity brings the awaited fulfillment of the quest: God completely revealed, not to the mind only, but to the whole man and to the universe from which he sprang.

In this Letter of St. John we have the proclamation of the fulfillment: Jesus is God. And this is completed by the declaration of the true order of reality: God is Love. St. John teaches but one truth: God is Love because He is completely One, Oneness Itself, and thus we must become One in Him. This is love, this is the meaningfulness of Christianity—awe-inspiring in its absoluteness. As Father, Son and Spirit are the singular Oneness of Divinity, so man must be one in the God of Love.

Not to love is the sin, the rebellion against God, the ultimate suicidal self-damnation. For God is the only source of reality, and to reject this One-All is to reject one's selfhood. This is true for every man, for every thing. Simply to exist, in the real sense, we must achieve unity within the One-All. We can reject nothing since all are one in Him.

The Church, the unity of mankind in Christ, exists to call all things into oneness: to love. Work is the act of love, worship is the act of love. Anything man can do, if it truly has meaning, must be the act of love. The individual seeks God through his life in the world, in the struggle of existence. With mind and heart each reaches out to God. We pray: asking, thanking, sorrowing, adoring—whatever the confrontation which living demands of us at the moment. But there is only one meaning to our prayer: the affirmation of the unity we have and seek in love. God is Love. Love is unity. Man seeks and so prays. He speaks in terms of the need of the moment, but, knowing it or not, what he says can have only one meaning.

In Christ, at last, man has seen God as He is—no longer

through images. In fact, because of Christ's transformation of all reality, there can be no images of God. He is All in all. The Christian must realize the sacredness of all beings: all within God—not just because they have come forth from Him but because they have returned. In Christ man and the universe have been made anew. We can find no more idols to worship. We cannot escape God Revealed.

Though we come upon ever new and deepening recognitions of the Revelation, the fullness of the theophany is to be found once and for all in Jesus. The Apostles beheld. And in this Letter to mankind St. John bears witness:

> Jesus is Christ
> Christ is God
> God is Love
> Love is One
> One is All

SAINT AUGUSTINE

In contrast to the Johannine texts, Augustine's writings reveal an orientation to formal philosophical conceptualization. Many passages from the *Confessions* emphasize a personal involvement with transcendence expressed in terms of changelessness and human limitation. The greater part of the *Confessions* deals with Augustine's reflective reactions to the experience of the divine, highlighted in the famous conversion scene with its interior theophany heralded by the mystic command, *"tolle, lege!"*

Augustine often stresses the Otherness in the relationship of the human as creature. The emphasis is on God as the absolute Reality, the explicitation of transcendence. He also reflects personalized experience of the limitation of reason, issuing in a discovery of the significance of transcendence, the last rational step leading to the mystical awareness of the Presence.

There is a marked difference between the Scriptural and philosophical statements reflecting transcendence. In the four centuries that separate the Johannine documents from the writings of Augustine a precision in analysis and terminology has been introduced into the expression of the Christian mysteries. Yet in the apprehended Presence there is the same awareness of the "All-Ruler" as Otherness—the "Lord God of the mind," "Most High," "unchangeable Truth," that is above yet within. Though Augustine conceptualizes something of the reality towards which he moves, it is to establish the limits of wisdom. Paradoxically, the limits become the sign for that which draws him beyond.

Augustine in speaking of the apprehension of the Presence in this life maintains a clear distinction between subject and object in union. The soul becomes a partaker in Truth but does not become Truth. He also speaks of the mystic as joined to God, as one spirit with God—all of which sounds like a fusion of the two. Yet this cannot be the writer's meaning in the light of other texts. Many passages from non-monist mystics seem to indicate fusion rather than union, but if evaluation is made in terms of total context and doctrinal commitments, we must deny monism. This difficulty in interpretation can best be seen in the history of Sufist mysticism which adheres to human-divine dualism and yet has often been accused of (and persecuted for) radical monism by orthodox Moslems.

The *Confessions* contain the most vivid material in Augustine's writings pertaining to union with God. Yet he is more concerned with the characteristics of the union he experiences than with the evaluation of the nature of the act. This provides us with a useful contrast to the material drawn from the Johannine Scriptures. Augustine lays special stress upon the dual aspect of permanency and transiency with regard to the union in its ultimate form after death as contrasted to its less perfect experience here and now. This is sharply expressed as not merely a union through concept by the use of the phrases, "snatched up

. . . but soon was snatched away," as well as the direct denial of a "mere phantasm" as the object of mystical love.

SAINT BERNARD OF CLAIRVAUX

In the *Sermons on the Canticle of Canticles* Bernard is attempting to instruct and inspire his monks, to move them with the significance and reality of mystical union. Besides establishing the Presence as transcendent, these texts serve as an introduction to the range of the mystical experience expressed by Bernard. Unlike Augustine, he does not seek here to relate the mystical state to abstractions of reason. Nor is his approach that of the Johannine Scriptures with their elusive feeling of timelessness. Rather, in Bernard there is a sense of urgency, a drive to convince others that they too must seek.

Bernard stresses the aspect of love in the mystic union, making extended use of the metaphor of marriage. In this he is, of course, drawing on symbolism that figures prominently in the Christian Scriptures—the wedding feast motifs, the exaltation of virginity in terms of a spiritual espousal, and, most important of all, the divine marriage of the Lamb in the Apocalypse. On the basis of this symbolism he draws a clear distinction between union and identification and rejects the latter as involved in the mystical state. However, the twoness "in one spirit" does not *explain* the mystery for him, because the union is still between two unequal persons.

Bernard concentrates on the marriage symbolism in many of these texts, often to the point of being too florid for modern taste. Yet this non-speculative mode of presentation allows us to judge the extent of the act of union to which he is attempting to draw his monks as well as the qualities of the act he claims to have experienced. In spite of the necessary emphasis on the mystic as an individual, it is of particular interest that he also clearly expresses the social context of the individual's participation in the mystical state. In the Christian theological and mystical tradition there is no such thing as the purely isolated individual. Insofar as the Christian is united to Christ, he is united to all others enjoying the same union. This involvement as a member of the Mystical Body of Christ (the Church in its inner meaning) necessarily pertains to the experience of Christ as the Presence. For the Christian mystic there is a great paradox: the more intense his experience of the Presence is—always in the incommunicable depths of the subject—the more he is united to all mankind, past, present and future. This view of the oneness achieved in the mystical act of divine love is a unifying theme running through all the Christian mystics and leading back to the Johannine proclamation of the divine essence: God is Love.

Bernard expresses the mystical state in "images of tangible things," "vessels of material of little worth." The transcendence of the Presence therefore appears as a contrast to the recognition of his own creaturehood. In this we can detect one of the most intriguing of the paradoxes of mysticism: awareness of transcendence through immanence. (This paradox might provide a clue to the interpretation of monist mysticism with its identification of the self as the Presence. The monist and non-monist *experience* of the mystical state could be the same, the only difference being the subjective evaluation given to the consciousness of the Presence as immanent: transcendent and other than self, or transcendent but actually the self. We shall see something of this when we explore ecumenical mysticism.)

SAINT JOHN OF THE CROSS

The approach of John of the Cross benefits from the fifteenth-century tradition of Christian mystical writers. We can see an accommodation of characteristics proper to the Johannine docu-

ments, Augustine and Bernard—doctrinal formularies, rational
relationships, the intimacy of the act of union as love. But John
of the Cross concentrates on the analysis of the elements of the
mystical state, stressing the limitations imposed by Faith and
reason, while insisting on the absoluteness of that which is to be
attained.

In Catholic doctrine man participates in God through grace,
that is, by means of a communication of divine existence. Man
remains a creature but is made to share in the divine mode of
existence. In attempting to express the absoluteness experienced
in the mystical state, John seems tempted to go far beyond participation. The realization of Presence is such as to suggest that
man's spirit is the God-head itself. This suggests the reason for
the difficulty some have found with this mystic as a Christian.
But the example of the window glass and ray of sunlight clearly
opposes a purely monist interpretation of his expression of transcendence.

John of the Cross goes more deeply into the problem of the
intimacy experienced in the mystical union than does Bernard
while using the same symbolism of spiritual marriage. It is evident that the selection of one or two passages from the *Spiritual
Canticle* or the *Living Flame of Love* could result in a total misinterpretation of the meaning given unification. When John
speaks of the deification of the soul he attempts to convey the
most radical meaning possible for a non-monist. Only when we
view these statements in the context of limits he sets, the proposal that the human is divine by participation while God is
divine by nature, can we avoid seeing deification as a destruction
of human nature in a transmutation of the creature into the
essence of the creator. Thus, John of the Cross proclaims mystical unification as an absorption, yet this is not identification in
which the subject realizes he *is* the Absolute. In some mysterious
way the human and the Presence are one and the distinction of
twoness remains.

Several passages introduce an item of great importance, the possibility of revelation in the mystical state. In the *high state of spiritual marriage* God reveals secrets of Himself and His works. Yet the mystic is quick to add that these revelations cannot be expressed, at least directly. We must note first that John is not saying that the mystical state is a revelation. Rather, such revelations that occur are results of the state and would form a part of the subjective experience of the state. What of the communication of such secrets? Here we have the question of the possible prophetic role of the mystic, keeping in mind the classic Old Testament duality of the prophetic office—the witness to God as Lord or the witness to revelations of God's will.

All four writers express certain common ideas on the dynamics of oneness that help to identify a specifically Christian tradition of mysticism as well as lay the groundwork for a comparison with other traditions. They each face the common problem of trying to express or conceptualize that which, by their own definition, is beyond concept.* It is possible to find and isolate texts to support almost any interpretation one cares to give mystical union. But adequate investigation of each writer reveals clearly that each maintains that union does not mean identification. If this were not the case (as often maintained in reference to John of the Cross) then each document from which we draw is grossly self-contradictory.

For the Christian mystic the union is brought about through

---

* The problem of conceptualization in terms of metaphysics-epistemology has been noted in the previously cited statement of St. Thomas: "The nature of God, however, cannot be seen by any created similitude representing the divine nature itself as it really is." (*S.Th.*, Pt.1, Q.12, A.2). We should be aware of the negative implications of this statement, viz., proper concepts of God are of the *divine nature itself as it really is not*. Although the so-called negative theology, of which this is certainly an expression, receives practically no emphasis in the Western theological tradition, this citation and the mystics' emphasis are elements in a convergence with Eastern Christian interest, exemplified in such Greek Fathers as Chrysostom.

the power (grace) of the Presence. The human is transformed, made god-like but *not Godhead*. Twoness remains in the extraordinary oneness of the state. From the beginning of the Christian tradition certain signs, especially those drawn from marriage, are used to typify the union. It is interesting to note the interplay of cultural limitations or determinations in reference to the marriage symbolism. The languages of the writers—Greek, Latin and Spanish—all render the word for *soul* as a feminine gender noun (*psyche, anima, alma*). Thus, the extended use of the nuptial metaphor is encouraged by the language (possibly even suggested by it) and not impeded as would be the case in English where the word is neuter, making it awkward to speak of the *soul* as *she*.

John of the Cross clearly views the act of union as a foretaste and foreshadowing of the perfect union of love to be expected after death. As with Bernard, these texts concentrate on the personal intimacy involved in the mystical act rather than on speculative characteristics. At the same time the texts go much further into the romantic symbolism prompted by the notion of the mystical state as a spiritual marriage. Regardless of the question of literary tastes, this symbolism leaves us with no doubt as to the interpretation given by John of the Cross to the state he experienced and the nature of the act of union.

All four Christian writers are in substantial agreement on the characteristics that constitute the subject's participation in the act. The act requires a giving of self to the Presence, focused in a surrender to the unifying love of the Word, the God-man, who is the only object to whom surrender can be made. Acceptance of this love entails a corresponding rejection of all other possible objects of desire. From this point on, creatures are not sought as ends but now serve as means to keep reminding the mystic that satiation of the thirst for love is to be found only in God.

The donation of self is accomplished through the act of the will, not by an intellectual grasp of the Presence. There is both an active and a passive aspect of the role of the will. Surrender can be made only with the prior communication of divine life—grace—which draws the subject to the Presence. Yet the subject must cooperate actively, especially in purifying and preparing himself. Most important of all, the subject must desire the union with his whole being. Thus, clearly, the act of union is not an accidental occurrence.

The writers emphasize the durational aspect of the mystical state in different ways. The actual encounter with the Presence is not permanent as can be seen in the contrast to the future life after death. Yet some distinguish between the intense act of union and a continuing state of unification, the former of short duration while the latter can be permanent.

It seems that the notion of a continuing though imperfect form of the mystical state should be seen as dependent upon two factors as far as Christian mystics are concerned. First, there is the doctrinal idea of grace, the communication of divine life enabling man to participate in the divine mode of existence —to have eternal life. Second, the experience of the Presence, as we should expect, involves a continuing emotional exaltation of the subject after the actual encounter is over. This factor of continuing after-effects is quite independent of any doctrinal considerations, and when we come to inquire into other mystical systems we can expect to find it an element held in common.

The Christian identification of God as Love itself provides the basis for the interpretation of the act of love as an act of Union. God is absolutely One—in fact, Oneness—and is love. Thus, to love God and be loved by Him means to be united as one. Whether we consider this in reference to the final consummation of man's life or the attempt to approach God directly here and now in the mystical state, this is the only meaning the Christian documents give to contact between the human and suprahuman. The Christian who accepts Jesus as the Son of God receives the Godhead as dwelling within him in a union of increasing intensity reaching perfection at death and possibly achieving the interior depth of the mystical state of union before. Upon this foundation of the interpretation of the basic human-suprahuman relationship the meaning given to all particular Christian experiences of mystical union rests.

First Johannine Letter*

REVELATION OF THE DIVINE UNITY (1:1-4)

That which was from the beginning
which we have heard
which we have seen with our eyes
which we have beheld
and our hands have touched:
of the Word of Life—
And the Life was revealed
and we have seen
and we bear witness
and we announce to you
the Eternal Life
which was with the Father
and was revealed to us—
That which we have seen and heard
we announce to you
so that you may have unity with us—
And truly our unity is with the Father
and with His Son Jesus Christ.

* The translation of this Letter is made from the Nestle Greek text of the
New Testament; for comparative purposes, cf. Nestle-Marshall, *The Interlinear
Greek-English New Testament* (London: Samuel Bagster and Sons, 1959).

And we write these things
that our joy may be fulfilled.

THE LIGHT OF TRUTH (1:5–10)

And this is the message
we have heard from Him and announce to you:
God is Light
and no darkness is in Him.
If we say that we have unity with Him
and walk in the darkness
we lie and do not practice the truth.
But if we walk in the light
we have unity with each other
and the Blood of Jesus His Son
cleanses us from all sin.
If we say we have no sin
we deceive ourselves
and the truth is not in us.
If we confess our sins
He is faithful and just
that He may forgive us our sins
and cleanse us from all our offenses.
If we say we have not sinned
we make Him a liar
and His Word is not in us.

UNITY IN THE COMMANDMENTS (2:1–6)

My little children,
I write these things to you
so that you do not sin.

And if anyone sins
we have an Advocate with the Father:
Jesus Christ the Just.
And He is a sacrifice for our sins
but not for ours only
but also for those of the whole world.
And by this we know that we have known Him:
if we keep His commandments.
He who says—I have known Him—
and does not keep His commandments
is a liar and the truth is not in him.
But whoever keeps His Word
truly in him the love of God has been perfected.
By this we know that we are in Him.
He who says he dwells in Him
ought himself so to walk as He walked.

THE GREAT COMMANDMENT (2:7-11)

Beloved, I do not write a new commandment to you
but an old commandment you had from the beginning,
the old commandment is the one you have heard.
Again, a new commandment I write to you
which is true in Him and in you
because the darkness passes
and the true light already shines.
He who says he is in the light
and hates his brother
is in the darkness even now.
He who loves his brother
dwells in the light
and there is no stumbling for him,

but he who hates his brother
is in the darkness
and walks in the darkness
and does not know where he goes
because the darkness has blinded his eyes.

THE FAITHFUL (2:12–14)

I write to you, little children,
because your sins have been forgiven you
for the sake of His Name.
I write to you, fathers,
because you have known Him
who is from the beginning.
I write to you, young men,
because you have overcome the evil one.
I have written to you, children,
because you have known the Father.
I have written to you, fathers,
because you have known Him
who is from the beginning.
I have written to you, young men,
because you are strong
and the Word of God dwells in you
and you have overcome the evil one.

THE PASSING OF THE OLD WORLD (2:15–17)

Do not love the world
nor the things in the world.
If anyone loves the world

the love of the Father
is not in him.
Because all that is in the world—
the desire of the flesh
and the desire of the eyes
and the vainglory of life—
is not of the Father
but is of this world.
And the world is passing away
and its desire,
but he who does the Will of God
remains forever.

THE SIGN OF THE CHRISTIAN (2:18–23)

Children, it is the last hour
and as you have heard
that Antichrist is coming,
so even now many antichrists have arisen
whereby we know it is the last hour.
They went out from us
but they were not of us—
for if they were of us
they would have remained with us—
but they went out
so that it might be shown
that none of them are of us.
And you have had an anointing from the Holy One
and you know all.
I do not write to you
because you do not know the truth

but because you know it
and because no lie is from the truth.
Who is the liar
if not the one who denies
that Jesus is the Christ?
He is the Antichrist
who denies the Father and the Son.
Everyone who denies the Son
has not the Father either,
but he who acknowledges the Son
also has the Father.

THE PROMISE OF LIFE (2:24–29)

That which you have heard from the beginning
let it dwell in you.
If that which you have heard from the beginning
dwells in you
you will dwell
both in the Son and in the Father.
And this is the promise that He promised us:
Eternal Life.
These things I have written to you
concerning those leading you astray.
And the anointing you have received from Him
dwells in you
and you have no need
that anyone teach you.
But as His anointing teaches you concerning all things
and is true and is not a lie,
and as it has taught you

so dwell in Him.
And now, little children, dwell in Him
that when He is revealed
we may have confidence
and not be ashamed before Him
at His Appearing.
And if you know that He is just
know also that everyone who practices justice
has been born of Him.

THE DIVINE PARENTAGE (3:1-2)

Behold what manner of love
the Father has given us
that we may be called
children of God—
and we are!
Therefore the world does not know us
because it did not know Him.
Beloved, now we are children of God
and it has not yet been shown
what we shall be.
We know that when He appears
we shall be like Him
because we shall see Him
as He is.

THE LIKENESS TO GOD (3:3-8)

And everyone who has this hope in Him
purifies himself as He is pure.

Everyone who commits sin also commits lawlessness
for sin is lawlessness.
And you know that He was revealed
that He might bear our sins
and sin is not in Him.
Whoever dwells in Him does not sin,
whoever sins has not seen Him
nor has known Him.
Little children, let no one lead you astray:
he who practices justice is just
as He is just.
He who commits sin is of the devil
because from the beginning the devil sins.
For this was the Son of God revealed
that He might undo the works of the devil.

CHILDREN ONE WITH ANOTHER (3:9–12)

Whoever has been begotten of God
does not commit sin
because His seed remains in Him
and he cannot sin
because he has been begotten of God.
In this the children of God are revealed
and the children of the devil also:
whoever does not practice justice
is not of God
nor is he who does not love his brother.
For this is the message you heard from the beginning
that we should love one another,
not as Cain who was the evil one

and slew his brother.
And why did he slay him?
Because his works were evil
while his brother's works were just.

LOVE IS LIFE (3:13-18)

Do not wonder, brothers, if the world hates you.
We know we have passed from death to life,
because we love our brothers—
he who does not love dwells in death.
Everyone who hates his brother is a murderer
and you know that no murderer
has eternal life dwelling in him.
By this we have known love:
because He laid down His life for us,
and we ought to lay down our lives for our brothers.
Whoever has the world's means of life
and sees that his brother has need
and shuts his heart from him—
how does the love of God dwell in Him?
Little children, let us not love in word or in tongue
but in work and in truth.

FAITH IS LOVE (3:19-24)

By this we shall know that we are of the truth,
and before Him we shall assure our hearts—
for if our heart accuses us
God is greater than our heart
and He knows all things.

Beloved, if our heart does not accuse us
we have confidence with God.
And whatever we ask
we receive from Him
because we keep His commandments
and do the things that are pleasing to Him.
And this is His commandment:
that we should believe in
the Name of His Son Jesus Christ
and love one another
as He gave us commandment.
And he who keeps His commandments
dwells in Him
and He in him.
And by this we know He dwells in us:
by the Spirit whom He has given to us.

TESTIMONY OF THE SPIRIT (4:1-6)

Beloved, do not believe every spirit,
but test if the spirits are of God
for many false witnesses
have gone forth into the world.
By this know the Spirit of God:
every spirit which witnesses
that Jesus Christ has come in the flesh,
is of God,
and every spirit which does not witness Jesus
is not of God—
and this is the spirit of the antichrist
which you have heard is coming

and is now already in the world.
You are of God, little children,
and have overcome them
because the One in you is greater
than the one in the world.
They are of the world
therefore they speak of the world
and the world hears them.
We are of God,
he who knows God hears us,
he who is not of God does not hear us.
From this we know
the spirit of truth
and the spirit of error.

GOD IS LOVE (4:7–8)

Beloved, let us love one another
because love is of God
and everyone who loves
has been begotten of God
and knows God.
He who does not love
does not know God
for God is Love.

GOD LOVES (4:9–10)

By this the love of God was revealed to us
because God has sent
His Only Begotten Son

into the world
that we might live through Him.
In this is love
not that we have loved God
but that He has loved us
and has sent His Son
as a sacrifice for our sins.

MAN LOVES (4:11–13)

Beloved, if God so loved us
we ought to love one another.
No man has ever seen God
but if we love one another
God dwells in us
and His love is made perfect in us.
By this we know
that we dwell in Him
and He in us
because He has given us His Spirit.

LOVE IS UNITY (4:14–16)

And we have beheld and bear witness
that the Father has sent the Son
as Savior of the world.
Whoever witnesses that Jesus is the Son of God
God dwells in him
and he in God.
And we have known and have believed
the love God has for us.

God is Love
and he who dwells in love
dwells in God
and God dwells in him.

LOVE IS ALL (4:17–19)

In this has love been perfected with us
that we may have confidence
in the day of judgment
because as He is
so also are we in this world.
There is no fear in love
but perfect love casts out fear
because fear has torment
and he who fears has not been perfected in love.
We love because He first loved us.

THE COMMANDMENT OF LOVE (4:20–21)

If anyone says—I love God—
and hates his brother,
he is a liar.
For he who does not love his brother
whom he has seen
cannot love God
whom he has not seen.
And this commandment we have from Him:
he who loves God
loves also his brother.

THE COMMANDMENT OF UNITY (5:1-3)

Everyone who believes Jesus is the Christ
has been begotten of God,
and everyone who loves Him who begot
loves him who has been begotten of Him.
By this we know that we love the children of God:
when we love God
and fulfill His commandments.
For this is the love of God:
that we keep His commandments,
and His commandments are not burdensome.

THE TRIUMPH OF FAITH (5:4-8)

For everything that has been begotten of God
overcomes the world
and this is the victory
that overcomes the world: our Faith.
And who is the one
who overcomes the world
but he who believes
that Jesus is the Son of God?
This is He who comes through water and blood,
Jesus Christ,
not by water only
but by water and by blood.
And the Spirit is the One who bears witness
because the Spirit is Truth.
Because there are three who witness:
the Spirit and the water and the blood
and the three are one.

THE DIVINE WITNESS (5:9-12)

If we accept the witness of men
the witness of God is greater
for this is the witness of God
because He has borne witness of His Son.
He who believes in the Son of God
has the witness in him.
He who does not believe God
has made Him a liar
because he has not believed in the witness
which God has borne concerning His Son.
And this is the witness:
that God gave us eternal life
and this life is in His Son.
He who has the Son has life—
He who does not have the Son of God
does not have life.

PRAYER FOR LOVE (5:13-15)

These things I have written to you
that you may know
that you have eternal life—
to those who believe
in the Name of the Son of God.
And this is the confidence we have toward Him
that if we ask anything
according to His will
He hears us.
And if we know that He hears us,
whatever we ask,

we know that we have the petitions
that we have sought from Him.

PRAYER OF LOVE (5:16-19)

If anyone sees his brother sinning
a sin which is not unto death,
he shall ask and he shall give him life,
to those not sinning unto death.
There is a sin unto death,
but I do not speak of it
that he should inquire into it.
All lawlessness is sin
and there is a sin not unto death.
We know that everyone begotten of God
does not sin,
but the Begotten of God preserves him
and the devil does not touch him.
We know we are of God
and the whole world
lies in the power of the evil one.

THE IMAGELESS GOD-MAN (5:20-21)

And we know the Son of God has come
and has given us understanding
that we might know the True One.
And we are in the True One,
in His Son Jesus Christ.
This is the true God and eternal life—
Little children,
guard yourselves from idols!

Saint Augustine*

CHANGELESS TRUTH

(The philosophers) understood well
that nobody could be God
and, thus, to find Him
they went beyond all material things.
Convinced that no changeable reality could be the Most High,
they transcended every soul and spirit subject to change
in their search for God.

(City of God, 8:6)

When judging of things visible
the human mind is able to know
that itself is better than all visible things.
But when, because of its failings and advances in wisdom,
it confesses itself to be changeable,
it discovers that above itself is the unchangeable Truth.

(De Diversis Quaestionibus, 83:45)

For He truly is because He is unchangeable:
for every change renders non-existent that which was.

(De Natura Boni, 19)

* The translations of the various passages have been made in the light of a number of available versions of which the following is most important: P. Schaff, ed., *A Select Library of the Nicene and Post-Nicene Fathers of the Christian Church* (Grand Rapids: Eerdmans Publishing Co., 1956).

CHANGELESS LIGHT

I strove as a man
—such as I was—
to think of You,
the highest and the only and the true God.
With my whole heart I believed
You are incorruptible and inviolable and immutable.

(Confessions, 7:1)

O God, Intelligible Light,
in whom and by whom and through whom
all things which possess intelligible light
have their intelligible light!

(Soliloquia, 1:3)

For you are the Lord God of the mind,
and all these things are mutable,
but you dwell above them all as an immutable Being.

(Confessions, 10:36)

GOD DWELLING

His dwelling-place is above my soul;
from there He beholds me,
from there He created me,
from there He directs me and makes provision for me,
from there He appeals to me,
calls me and directs me,
leads me in the way
and to the end of my way . . .

(Enarrationes in Psalmos, 41:7)

God is not seen in any place,
but in the pure heart.
He is not sought by bodily eyes,
nor limited by our sight,
nor held by touch,
nor heard by His utterance,
nor perceived in His approach.
When He is thought absent,
He is seen,
when He is present,
He is not seen.

(*De Videndo Deo*, 147:52)

He is in the depths of the heart,
but the heart has strayed from Him.
Return into your heart, O sinners,
and cleave to Him who has made you.

(*Confessions*, 4:18)

THE SEARCH WITHIN

And behold you were within
and I was without.
I was searching for you there,
and I cast myself, deformed as I was,
upon those well-formed things that you have made.
You were within me,
but I was not with you.

(*Confessions*, 10:38)

Your words had clung tightly within the depths of my heart,
and I was fenced in on all sides by you.

(*Confessions*, 8:1)

You were deeper within me than my innermost depths
and higher than my highest parts.

(Confessions, 3:11*)*

Who is there to instruct me
except Him who enlightens my heart
and sees through its shadows?

(Confessions, 2:16*)*

For the Lord is a spirit.
Therefore, "he who is joined to the Lord is one spirit."
Consequently, he who can see God invisibly
can be joined to God incorporeally.

(De Videndo Deo, 147:37*)*

The unchangeable Truth shines like a sun in the soul,
and the soul becomes partaker of the Truth itself.

(De Genesi ad Litteram, 1:43*)*

VISION

And in this life the highest spiritual state of the soul
consists in the vision and contemplation of Truth,
in which are joys and the complete enjoyment of the highest
    and truest Good,
and a breath of serenity and eternity,
such as some great and incomparable souls have described to
    some extent
and who, we believe, have seen and do see such things.

(De Quantitate Animae, 76*)*

For God causes those visions in which He appears
as He wills,
to whom He wills
and when He wills,
while His substance remains hidden and unchangeable in itself.
If our will, as it remains in itself
and without any change in itself,
expresses words through which it manifests itself after a fashion,
how much more easily can the Omnipotent God,
while keeping His nature hidden and unchangeable,
appear under any form He wills and to whom He wills,
since He made all things out of nothing,
and, remaining in Himself, "renews all things."

　　　　　　　　　　　(*De Videndo Deo*, 147:47)

GOD BEYOND MIND

When people are frightened and overwhelmed
by apprehension of temporal difficulties,
you well know how this type of reasoning brings relief,
namely, that the mind and understanding are superior
to the eyes and the ordinary sense of sight.
Such would not be the case
unless the things we understand are superior
to those we perceive by the senses.
I ask you to consider with me
if there be anything opposed to this reasoning.
After I had taken comfort in it for some time
and after I had called upon God for help,
I began to be lifted up to Him
and to those things that are most completely true.

I was so penetrated with a knowledge of eternal things
that I wondered how I had ever needed to reason about them
since they are as intimately present as a man is to himself.

(Letter to Nebridius, 4:2)

And this (intellectual) power,
also finding itself changeable in me,
elevated itself to its understanding
and withdrew the thinking process from the customary level . . .
And, in the flash of a trembling glance,
it reached up to That Which Is.

(Confessions, 7:23)

FOUNTAIN OF LIFE

. . . "As the hart desires the watery streams,
so does my spirit long after You, O God."
Who is it, then, who says this?
Ourselves, if we be but willing!

(Enarrationes in Psalmos, 41:1)

"With God is the fountain of Life,"
a fountain that shall never run dry;
in His Light there is a Light that shall never be darkened.
Long for this Light:
for a certain fountain
and a certain light
such as your bodily eyes do not know.
A light to see
for which the inward eye must be prepared;
a fountain to drink of
for which the inward thirst must be aroused.

Run to the fountain,
long for the fountain!
But do not do it just any way,
do not be satisfied with running like any ordinary animal—
run like the hart!
What is meant by "like the hart"?
Let there be no sloth in your running.
Run with all your might.
Long for the fountain with all your might.
For we find in the hart the emblem of swiftness.

(*Enarrationes in Psalmos*, 41:2)

CONTEMPLATION

... and eternal life consists in that contemplation
in which God is seen,
not for punishment
but for everlasting joy ...

(*De Trinitate*, XV, 1:31)

Therefore Our Lord Jesus Christ
will so give over the kingdom to God the Father,
Himself not being thence excluded nor the Holy Spirit,
when He shall bring believers to the contemplation of God
wherein is the end of all good actions,
and everlasting rest and joy
which will never be taken away from us.

(*De Trinitate*, XV, 1:20)

I marveled that I now loved You
and not a mere phantasm in place of You.
Yet I did not stand still in the enjoyment of my God.

Rather, I was snatched up to You by Your Glory,
but soon was snatched away from You
by the natural weight of my will,
and I fell back on these lower things with a groan.
This was the weight of carnal habit.

(Confessions, 7:23)

PURIFICATION

"I shall know You,"
O Knower of mine,
"I shall know You
just as I have been known."
Virtue of my soul,
go deep into it
and make it fit for You,
that You may have and possess it
"without spot or wrinkle."
This is my hope
and that is why I speak,
and in this "hope I rejoice,"
when my joy is well-founded.

(Confessions, 10:1)

. . . O happy and secure Sweetness,
who gathers me in from the dispersion
in which I was divided and cut off—
when I turned away from Your Unity
and wasted myself on the many.

(Confessions, 2:1)

Such a spirit is not renewed in a man
unless first his heart shall have been purified,
that is, unless he restrain his thoughts
and draw them away from all worldly attachment and
    defilement.

(*De Quantitate Animae, 75*)

UNIFICATION

... You have delivered me from all my worst ways
so that You might become more sweet to me
than all other attractions which I was seeking.

(*Confessions, 1:24*)

In all simplicity I now dare say this to you
that, providing we hold with all perseverance
to the course God lays down for us
and which we have understanding to hold,
we shall come by God's Power and Wisdom
to that highest Cause or Supreme Author
or Supreme Principle of all things,
or whatever other name you would deem worthy
of so great a Reality.

(*De Quantitate Animae, 76*)

You have made us for Yourself
and our heart is restless
until it finds its rest in You.

(*Confessions, 1:1*)

FROM THE DEPTH

O Truth, Light of my heart,
let not my darkness speak to me!
I slipped down to these things
and was darkened,
but from there, from that depth itself,
I fell in love with You.
I have gone astray
but I have not forgotten You.

(Confessions, 12:10)

I love You, O Lord,
not with a doubtful but with an assured awareness.
You have pierced my heart with Your Word,
and I have loved You.
Heaven and earth and all that are in them—
see how in every way they tell me to love You!

(Confessions, 10:8)

LIFE ALIVE

... O God, Light of my heart
and Bread of the inner mouth of my soul,
O virile Power who espouses my mind
and the bosom of my thought!

(Confessions, 1:21)

Look at my heart, O God,
look at my heart which You have pitied
in the depths of the abyss.

(Confessions, 2:9)

Let me love You with all my strength,
let me cling to Your Hand with all my heart strings,
and I shall be delivered from all temptations
even to the end.

(Confessions, 1:24)

When I shall cleave to You with all my being,
sorrow and toil will exist no longer for me
and my life will be alive,
wholly filled with You.

(Confessions, 10:39)

Saint Bernard of Clairvaux*

ALL IN ALL

We search for
that which the eye has never seen,
that which the ear has never heard,
that which has not come into the thought of any man.
It is that which will delight us,
and that which we desire,
that, whatever it may be,
for which we joyfully search.
They say, "God will enlighten them interiorly,
and He will be all things in all."
This which I expect,
the plenitude we await from God,
will be nothing else but God Himself.

(*Canticle of Canticles,* 11:4)

... following the example of Scripture
which comes into our words
to express the wisdom hidden in this mystery,
and which, in order to portray God to our spirits,

* The translations of the various passages generally follow the text and interpretation of Abbé Charpentier, *Oeuvres Complètes de S. Bernard de Clairvaux* (Paris: Librairie de Louis Vives, 1866).

presents Him through images of tangible things
giving us thus a precious advantage:
I wish to speak of that of God
which is unknown and invisible,
in vessels of material of little worth.

(*Canticle of Canticles*, 74:2)

WISDOM

What is God?
God is all-powerful will,
infinite goodness and strength,
eternal light,
unchangeable cause
and supreme beatitude ...

(*De Consideratione*, 5:24)

God is wisdom.
He does not wish to be loved only with gladness,
but with wisdom.

(*Canticle of Canticles*, 19:7)

... if we consider Him in Himself,
He dwells in inaccessible light (I Tim., 6:16).
His peace surpasses all that can be imagined (Philip., 4:1).
His wisdom does not have boundaries,
nor His grandeur limits,
and no man is able to see Him in this life (Exod., 33:29).

(*Canticle of Canticles*, 4:4)

DIVINE SPOUSE

One who does not dare to claim
a pure heart, a good conscience, a sincere faith,
says, "He pays attention to me!"
Is it possible that such a high Majesty,
who has charge of the government and conduct of the universe,
deigns to care for her?
That the God of the ages
is occupied not only with great things
but with the tranquility
of the love and desires of the spouse?
This, in effect, is the case.

(Canticle of Canticles, 68:2)

"My beloved to me,
and I to Him."
There is not liaison in this
and we should not be astonished;
it is an effusion of hearts.

(Canticle of Canticles, 67:4)

You see to what extent the soul is elevated,
and to what heights comes a soul
who has the right to call the Lord of the universe
her beloved.
Note, in effect, that she does not say simply "Beloved,"
but "my Beloved,"
to signify that He is her very own.

(Canticle of Canticles, 45:6)

ONE SPIRIT

Bring chaste ears to this discourse of love,
and when you think of these two lovers
do not think of a man and a woman,
but the Word and the soul,
or better, Jesus Christ and the Church,
which is the same thing,
except that this term Church
indicates not a single soul
but the unity
or rather the union of several souls.

(*Canticle of Canticles*, 61:2)

Behold a marriage contract
which is truly sacred and spiritual.
Not only that, it is not a contract,
it is an embrace, yes, an embrace,
for the perfect union of their wills
makes only one spirit out of two.

(*Canticle of Canticles*, 83:3)

She is His sister
because she has the same Father as He.
She is His spouse
because she has the same spirit.
For if a carnal marriage establishes two persons in one flesh,
why should not spiritual marriage
unite them rather in one spirit?

(*Canticle of Canticles*, 8:9)

SPIRITUAL MARRIAGE

   . . . there is a place where we see God
truly at rest and tranquil;
it is the place not of a judge or of a Master,
but that of a Spouse.

(Canticle of Canticles, 23:15)

And when she will have become perfect,
He will contract a spiritual marriage with her,
and they will be two,
not in flesh
but in one spirit
according to the word of the Apostle:
"He who is truly united to God
is but one spirit with Him" (I Cor., 6:17)

(Canticle of Canticles, 61:1)

The torrents of love and of the loved,
of the soul and of the Word,
of the bride and of the Bridegroom,
of the Creator and of the creature,
of him who thirsts and of the fountain
which quenches the thirst—
these do not flow with equal abundance.

(Canticle of Canticles, 83:6)

THE WORD AND THE SOUL

   "My beloved to me,
and I to Him."
Without doubt we see in this passage

an ardent and reciprocal love of two persons,
one for the other.
But in this love shines the happiness of the one
and the marvelous goodness of the other.
For this close union of love
is not between two equal persons.

(Canticle of Canticles, 67:8)

And there is no sweeter expression
to portray the reciprocal friendship of the Word and the soul,
than that of spouse;
since all is common between them
and they possess nothing of their own or separately.
They have the same heritage,
the same house,
the same table,
the same bed,
the same flesh.

(Canticle of Canticles, 7:2)

ONE IN THE OTHER

But we believe that God and man
dwell one in the other
in a way very different
because they each have their own substance and will,
and exist separately one in the other.
In other words,
we believe that there is never confusion of substances,
but agreement of wills,

their union is a likeness of willing
and conformity of love.

(Canticle of Canticles, 71:10)

. . . there certainly is difference
between the essence of God and that of man,
but on the other hand
the essence of the Father and Son is one.
Do you think that this unity,
that of man with God,
is strictly speaking one,
when we compare it with this other
unique and sovereign unity?
For how can there be unity
where there is plurality of nature
and difference of substance?
Nonetheless a soul who adheres to God
is called and is, in effect,
one same spirit with Him,
and the plurality of essences does not prejudice this unity
since it is not formed by a confusion of natures
but by an agreement of wills.

(Canticle of Canticles, 71:7)

GLORY

To be carried into the clouds,
to penetrate the fullness of light,
to pierce the abyss of splendors
and inhabit inaccessible light,

these are things which are not possible
as long as you are still mortal flesh.
This happiness is reserved for you
for the end of time,
when I shall cause you to appear before Me,
clothed in glory,
with neither stain nor wrinkle,
exempt from every other defect whatever it may be.

(Canticle of Canticles, 38:5)

THE SEARCH

I also reached above myself
and I found that the Word is still higher.
My curiosity led me to search for Him below me,
and I found likewise that He is still lower.
I looked outside myself,
and I realized that He is still beyond
that which is outside me.
And at last I searched within,
and I saw that He is still more interior to me
than myself.

(Canticle of Canticles, 74:5)

My soul searches for the Word,
but He has sought her first.

(Canticle of Canticles, 84:3)

As I said, the motive of the love of God
is God Himself,
and I have good reason to say it;

He is in effect the cause,
at the same time efficient and final,
of our love.
For it is He who has brought forth
the occasion of love,
He who has enflamed the ardor
and He who has aroused the desires.

(*De Diligendo Deo*, 22)

... contemplation can come
only from the grace of God,
never from the will of man.

(*Sermones de Diversis*, 87:3)

CHRIST LIFE

Note that in spiritual marriage
there are two kinds of child-bearing
and consequently two kinds of children
which, without being contradictory, are different:
for holy mothers bring souls to God through preaching,
or produce spiritual intellects through meditation.
In one, she is pressed by care of her neighbor;
in the other she is clothed with the sweetness of the Word.
She is a mother who has truly much joy
in bringing forth spiritual children,
but who prefers the chaste embrace of her Spouse.
Her children are dear and precious to her,
but the kisses of the Spouse
are infinitely more agreeable.
It is a good thing to save several souls,
but it is much sweeter to be wrapped out of oneself,

and to be with the Word.
But when this happens how long does it last?
It is a sweet communication,
but it is very short when one experiences it,
and it is very rarely experienced.

(Canticle of Canticles, 85:13)

When you see one who after having left everything
is attached to the Word with all desires of her heart,
lives only for the Word,
acts through the Word,
conceives by the Word to bear fruit for the Word,
so that she may say:
"Jesus Christ is my life,
and to die for Him is gain for me" (Philip., 1:21),
then you may say she is the spouse of the Word.

(Canticle of Canticles, 85:12)

THE COMING

. . . she wishes that, by a special privilege,
He would come down to her
from the height of heaven,
that He penetrate her intimately
and to the depth of her heart.
She wishes that He whom she desires
would not show Himself to her under an exterior form
but that He come as an infusion into her,
not that He appear to her
but that He penetrate her,
for one cannot doubt

that He is more delightful within than without.
For the Word does not resound
in the ears
but pierces the heart.
It is not loquacious
but efficacious.
It does not make noise
but It is sweet to the soul.
It is a face
which does not have form
but which forms,
which does not strike the eyes of the body
but which fills the heart with joy,
which love rather than exterior beauty makes delightful.

(Canticle of Canticles, 31:6)

Not being able to see
the pain of His spouse,
He comes before her.
For He is not able to delay longer
when He is called by such ardent desires.

(Canticle of Canticles, 51:5)

THE DWELLING

I do not know how it is with others,
but for me it is a room
where sometimes it comes to me to enter;
but, alas, it happens rarely
and then I dwell there only a short time.

(Canticle of Canticles, 23:15)

. . . if you persevere in knocking at this door,
you will not come away with empty hands.
And when you return to us
full of grace and love,
ardent and beloved,
you will not be able to conceal
the gift you have received . . .

(Canticle of Canticles, 49:3)

If the devoted soul
continues to pray and to sigh,
He will return to her,
not depriving her of the fruit of her prayers,
but presently He disappears
and does not return
until she seeks Him again
with all the desires of her heart.

(Canticle of Canticles, 32:2)

PRAYER

   I believe it is now easy
to relate the four types of prayer
to four expressions used by the Apostle,
for we grasp the length
by meditation on the promises,
the width
by remembrance of benefits,
the height
by contemplation of the Divine Majesty,

the depth
by perceiving the judgments of God.

(*De Consideratione*, 5:32)

The Lord has two feet:
these are mercy and truth.
God impresses His two feet
on the hearts of those who turn to Him,
and every sinner who is converted
sincerely embraces these two feet.
For if he receives only mercy without truth,
he falls into presumption;
so also if he receives truth without mercy,
he inevitably perishes of despair.

(*Sermones de Diversis*, 87:1)

DESIRE

I admit I have received favors
which are much above my merits,
but they are beneath my desires.
I am led by my desires;
it is not reason which guides me.
Do not accuse me of temerity, I beg of you,
for that which is only the effect of an ardent love.

(*Canticle of Canticles*, 9:2)

God is not sought
by a movement of the feet
but by desire.

(*Canticle of Canticles*, 84:1)

Each soul to whom He would come
must anticipate His coming
by such ardent desires
that they will consume
all the impurity of his vices
and thus prepare a place for the Lord.

(Canticle of Canticles, 31:4)

FIDELITY

It is not to another than Him,
no matter who,
be it angel or man,
but it is to Himself
that I make the request
that He kiss me
with a kiss of His mouth.

(Canticle of Canticles, 2:2)

Her spouse may repose in her with confidence,
knowing that the soul who has disdained all
for love of Him
and who regards all as nothing
to gain and possess Him uniquely,
is faithful to Him.

(Canticle of Canticles, 85:12)

THE WHOLE HEART

... you have separated (the Spouse) from you
by an infinity of walls,

of which the first is concupiscence,
the second is consent,
the third is the act,
the fourth is the habit
and the fifth is contempt . . .

(Canticle of Canticles, 56:6)

It is not that one cannot love
Jesus Christ in the flesh
without the Holy Spirit,
but one cannot love Him thus fully.
And in any case,
the measure of this love
is that the sweetness which is born of it
occupy the whole heart,
drawing it entirely from the love of tangible creatures,
and cutting it from the charms
and attractions of carnal pleasure,
because that is what it means
to love with one's whole heart.

(Canticle of Canticles, 20:7)

Does it not seem to you that she means to say:
"What is there in heaven or on earth
capable of being the object of my desires
besides you?" (Ps. 67:25)
She surely loves chastely
who seeks only Him whom she loves,
without concerning herself with anything other than Him.

(Canticle of Canticles, 7:3)

UNION

Contemplation occurs through the abasement
of the Word of God toward human nature,
with the aid of grace
and with the elevation of human nature
toward the Word,
with the assistance and the love of God.

(*Sermones de Diversis,* 87:3)

It is by agreement of wills
that they are two in one spirit,
or rather that they are only one spirit.

(*Canticle of Canticles,* 71:8)

. . . it is a nuptial song
which expresses chaste and sweet spiritual embraces,
a perfect union of wills,
and a bond of affection
and mutual inclinations.

(*Canticle of Canticles,* 1:11)

THE CHURCH

What familiarity do you think this habitation produces
between the soul and the Word,
and what confidence is not born of this familiarity?
I believe that such a soul is able to say without fear:
"My Beloved to me";
for knowing that she loves God
and that she loves Him with a violent love,

she does not doubt
that she is also passionately loved.

(*Canticle of Canticles,* 69:7)

. . . these things are not only for the Church,
for each one of us
who together comprise this same Church
must participate also in these blessings.

(*Canticle of Canticles,* 57:3)

Saint John of the Cross*

THE SEEKING

First, it must be known
that if a soul is seeking God,
its Beloved is seeking it much more.
And if it sends its loving desires after Him—
these are as fragrant to Him
as a pillar of smoke
arising from the aromatic spices
of myrrh and incense—
He likewise sends after it
the fragrance of His unguents,
with which He attracts the soul
and causes it to run after Him.

(*Living Flame of Love*, 3:38)

Therefore in this state
the soul can perform no acts,
but it is the Holy Spirit that performs them

* The translations of the various passages are based on the edition of the texts of Silverio de Santa Teresa, C.D. (published in Burgos, 1929–31). For the complete English text, the reader is referred to the standard English translations of E. Allison Peers, *Complete Works of St. John of the Cross, Doctor of the Church* (London: Burns, Oates and Washbourne, Ltd., revised edition, 1953).

and moves it to perform them.
Therefore all its acts are divine
since it is impelled and moved to them by God.

(*Living Flame of Love*, 1:4)

TRANSFORMATION

And this breathing of the Holy Spirit in the soul,
by which God transformed it into Himself,
is such a sublime and delicate and profound delight to it
that it cannot be described by mortal tongue,
nor is human understanding as such
able to reach any conception of it.

(*Spiritual Canticle*, 39:3)

And this is the great delight of this awakening:
to know creatures through God
and not God through creatures,
to know the effects through their cause
and not the cause through the effects;
for the latter knowledge is secondary
and this other is essential.

(*Living Flame of Love*, 4:5)

GRACE AND UNION

In this breathing of the Holy Spirit through the soul,
which is His visitation of her in love,
the Spouse, who is the Son of God,
communicates Himself to her in an exalted way.

(*Spiritual Canticle*, 17:8)

But in this matter it must be noted clearly
that a difference exists
between the possession of God through grace alone
and the possession of Him through union.
For the one is a question of mutual love
and the other is one of communication.
There is as great a difference between these states
as there is between betrothal and marriage.

(*Living Flame of Love*, 3:24)

SPIRITUAL MARRIAGE

This (spiritual marriage)
is incomparably far greater
than the spiritual betrothal
because it is a total transformation
in the Beloved,
in which on either side surrender is made
by total possession
of the one to the other
with a certain consummation
of union of love,
in which the soul is made divine
and becomes God by participation,
so far as this can be in this life.
And so I think that this state is never attained
without the soul being confirmed in grace.
For the faithfulness of both is confirmed,
that of God being confirmed in the soul.
Therefore this is the highest state
attainable in this life.

For, even as in the consummation of marriage
according to the flesh
the two become one flesh as Holy Scripture says,
even so when this spiritual marriage is consummated
between God and the soul,
there are two natures
in one spirit and love.

(*Spiritual Canticle*, 22:3)

REVELATION

In this high state of spiritual marriage
the Spouse reveals His wonderful secrets to the soul ...
He communicates principally to it
sweet mysteries concerning His Incarnation
and the modes and ways of human redemption,
which is one of the highest works of God,
and thus is most delightful to the soul.

(*Spiritual Canticle*, 23:1)

For who can write what He reveals
to the loving souls in whom He dwells?
And who can set forth in words
that which He causes them to feel?
Finally, who can express
that which He makes them desire?
Unquestionably no one!
No indeed, not the very souls
through whom He passes.

(*Spiritual Canticle*, Prologue: 1)

INFUSION OF LOVE

... for in the way of nature
it is not possible to love
if one does not first understand
that which one is to love.
But in the supernatural way
God can readily infuse love
and can increase it
without infusing or increasing distinct knowledge ...
Those spiritual persons
who have not a very excellent understanding of God
habitually excel in will,
and infused faith
rather than intellectual knowledge
is sufficient for them ...

(Spiritual Canticle, 26:8)

The soul then desires to see herself possessed
by this great God,
by whose love the heart feels itself
stolen away and wounded ...

(Spiritual Canticle, 11:2)

GREAT LOVE

... for as much as the desire
with which she seeks Him
is genuine
and her love is great,
she is unwilling to leave unmade

any effort within her power.
For the soul that truly loves God
is not slothful in doing its utmost
to find the Son of God,
its Beloved.
And even after having done everything
it is still not satisfied
and thinks that it has done nothing.

(*Spiritual Canticle*, 3:1)

. . . for it must proceed
with such love and solicitude
that it does not rest the foot of its desire
upon the green bough of any delight,
nor desire to drink the clear water
of any honor or glory of the world,
nor must it desire to taste the coolness
of any temporal consolation or refreshment,
nor desire to stay beneath the shade
of any favor or protection that is from creatures;
in no way desiring to take rest in anything
or to find companionship in other affections,
and always sighing for solitude from all things
until it finds its Spouse in complete satisfaction.

(*Spiritual Canticle*, 34:5)

REBIRTH IN THE SPIRIT

. . . such favors cannot be received
by one who is wholly in the flesh,
for the spirit is elevated
to commune with the Divine Spirit

that comes to the soul,
and thus in some manner it must abandon the flesh.

(Spiritual Canticle, 13:4)

. . . to be born again
in the Holy Spirit in this life
is to possess a soul most like God in purity,
having in itself no admixture of imperfection,
so that a pure transformation
can be brought about in it
through participation of union,
although not essentially.

(Ascent of Mount Carmel, II, 5:5)

And so, having removed from it
once and for all
sin and foulness,
He never again looks at them,
nor on their account
does He fail to grant the soul more favors,
since He does not judge the same thing twice.
Yet, though God forgets the evil and sin
after He has once pardoned them,
the soul in no way must consign
its first sins to oblivion . . .

(Spiritual Canticle, 33:1)

GLORIOUS MARRIAGE

Therefore the soul may well know
if it loves God purely or not.
For if it loves Him

it will have no heart for itself
nor for regarding its own pleasure and profit,
but only for the honor and glory of God
and for giving Him pleasure,
because the more of its heart
it reserves for itself,
the less it has for God.

(Spiritual Canticle, 9:5)

She says that her soul and her body
and her faculties and all her abilities
are no longer occupied in other things
but in those that pertain to the service of her Spouse.

(Spiritual Canticle, 28:2)

The Bride sets all these perfections and dispositions
before her Beloved, the Son of God,
with the desire to be transported by Him
from the Spiritual Marriage
to which God has been pleased to bring her
in this Church Militant,
to the Glorious Marriage
of the Church Triumphant . . .

(Spiritual Canticle, 40:7)

THIS LIFE

. . . with the Divine favor,
there can be no permanent union in the faculties in this life,
but only a transitory union.

(Ascent of Mount Carmel, II, 5:2)

And so that this thirsty soul
may come to find her Spouse
and be united with Him in this life
through the union of love—
so far as she may—
and slake her thirst with this drop
that can be tasted of Him in this life . . .

(*Spiritual Canticle,* 1:6)

. . . as I say, this is love's sweetness in the soul.
At times it lasts for a day or two;
at other times for many days,
but not always at the same degree of intensity,
since it weakens or increases
and the soul is not able to control it.

(*Spiritual Canticle,* 25:8)

DESIRE

There can be no medicine for the wounds of love
except that which comes from Him who dealt the wounds.

(*Spiritual Canticle,* 1:20)

It is to be noted here
that any soul who truly loves
cannot wish to achieve satisfaction and contentment
until she truly possesses God.
For not only do all other things
fail to satisfy her,
but also as we have said

they increase her hunger and desire
to see Him as He is.

(Spiritual Canticle, 6:4)

PARTICIPATION

... wherein such union of the two natures
and such communication
of the Divine Nature to the human is brought about
that, while neither of them changes its being,
each of them appears to be God.
Although this cannot come to pass perfectly in this life,
yet it surpasses everything
that can be described or conceived.

(Spiritual Canticle, 22:4)

Thus, souls possess these same blessings by participation
as He possesses them by nature;
therefore they are truly gods by participation,
equals of God,
and His companions.

(Spiritual Canticle, 39:6)

... and the soul appears to be God
instead of a soul,
and, indeed, it is God by participation—
although it is true that its natural being
(though thus transformed)
is as distinct from the Being of God
as it was before,
just as the window-pane has a nature distinct

from that of the light-ray,
though the ray gives it its brightness.

(Ascent of Mount Carmel, II, 5:7*)*

Thus, it is to be noted that,
however lofty in this life
are the communications of a soul with God
and the revelations of His presence,
and however high and exalted
is its knowledge of Him,
these are not God in His Essence,
nor do they have anything to do with Him.
For actually He is still hidden from the soul.

(Spiritual Canticle, 1:3*)*

LIKENESS TO GOD

The Bride calls Him "Beloved"
in order to move and incline Him
even more to her prayer,
because when God is loved
He responds with great readiness
to the petitions of His lover.

(Spiritual Canticle, 1:13*)*

For usually the favors and visitations
of God to the soul
are great in proportion
to the fervors and yearnings of love
that have preceded them.

(Spiritual Canticle, 13:2*)*

... the union and transformation of the soul with God,
which is not being brought about continuously
but only when that likeness is produced
which comes from love,
comes about when the two wills—
that of the soul and that of God—
are conformed together in one,
and there is nothing in the one
that is repugnant to the other.

(Ascent of Mount Carmel, II, 5:3)

... that the Spouse might enter,
she (is) keeping open the door of the will for Him
with the true and complete consent of love,
which is the consent of the betrothal
given before the Spiritual Marriage.

(Spiritual Canticle, 21:2)

ONE LIFE

The soul says that He dwells secretly in its breast
because, as we have said,
this sweet embrace is made
in the depth of the substance of the soul.

(Living Flame of Love, 4:14)

This kiss is the union of which we speak,
in which the soul is made equal with God
through love.

(Spiritual Canticle, 24:5)

Such are the encounters
with which He penetrates the soul continually,
deifying its substance
and making it divine,
in which the Being of God
absorbs the soul above all being.

(Living Flame of Love, 1:35)

And it is of this degree of enkindled love
that the soul must be understood as speaking
when at last it is so far transformed
and perfected interiorly in the fire of love
that not only is it united with this fire,
but it has become now one living flame within it.

(Living Flame of Love, Prologue: 4)

Thus, according to this likeness of transformation,
we can say that one's life
and the life of Christ
were one life
through the union of love,
which will be accomplished perfectly in heaven.

(Spiritual Canticle, 12:8)

THE HIDDEN WORD

Last of all, then,
O You ineffably delicate Touch,
You are the Word
who does not touch the soul

except with Your most pure and simple Being
which, being infinite, is infinitely delicate
and therefore touches
most subtly, lovingly, eminently and delicately.

(Living Flame of Love, 2:20)

Come, then, beautiful soul,
since now you know that the Beloved of your desire
dwells hidden within your bosom,
strive to be hidden securely with Him,
and in your bosom you shall embrace Him
and experience His presence
with affection and love.

(Spiritual Canticle, 1:10)

FOUR

Non-Christian Mysticism

If comparisons are odious, it would seem that comparisons of religious traditions are most odious of all. For religion is one aspect of conscious life that demands and actually achieves a state of personal commitment from every man. Religion evokes life-commitment for or against, this latter including the strange commitment to indifference. Each is a real commitment, for from each comes a pattern of life reflecting the recognition (or denial) of relations between man—*this* man—and Something Else. But religion does not exist in the abstract except for purposes of theoretical analysis. Hence, religious commitment is for or against specific systems of religion. Commitment to one system often implies commitment against others, and one may be committed against all systems or indifferent to all. In any case, personal involvement must show itself in any attempt at comparison, and thus all comparisons are in danger of distortion.

But this danger is real not only in the sense of a subjective commitment to one system casting a negative evaluation on others. As religion does not exist in the abstract but as concrete systems to which people are committed, then can any religious system be understood fully unless the force of commitment is accounted for? While admitting that it cannot, we still hope that comparative studies can be designed within disciplinary limits providing an adequate understanding of the non-subjective aspects of the systems.

Within a specifically theological framework, a comparison of Christian with non-Christian systems usually is far from indifferent as to commitment. In the past, certainly, this type of study would be characterized by such polemic terms as "infidel," "pagan," "heathen," and worse, and the purpose of such study would be to "refute" the supposed validity of non-Christian systems and demonstrate that whatever "natural truth" lies outside historic Christendom is overshadowed by "superstition," "idolatry," "immorality," and a general perverse blindness to truth. This was not the theological approach in the early Patristic period, with the interest of such Fathers as Justin Martyr and Clement of Alexandria centered on "Christianizing" the great figures and philosophic systems of the Graeco-Roman world. Unfortunately, interest has been confined almost exclusively within the cultural boundaries of that world, at least until recently.

The rise and sudden popularization of Christian ecumenism and its almost inescapable extension to non-Christian religious traditions calls for a reversal of theological attitude. It is no longer possible simply to reject what we find outside our tradition, but it is also not possible to treat the other traditions with some sort of neutral academic interest. Theological ecumenism necessitates the development of an appropriately systematized synthesis of mankind's long and many-sided quest that has given rise to the literally thousands of religious forms.

Synthesis is the crucial term, implying opposition both to indifferentism and syncretism. Each lurks beyond the outer limits of genuine ecumenism. Each can appear as the logical conclusion of the ecumenical process. But each, in reality, is a nullification of the organic unification towards which ecumenism is oriented.

All of these issues must be noted at the outset of our inquiry into some of the materials of non-Christian mystical systems, but consideration of them must be left to the concluding chapter. The issues are raised here to clarify the approach taken in presenting the selections from the texts of mysticism. In terms of the theoretical analysis of mysticism, the mystical process and state as presented in the opening chapters, we must make and constantly be aware of the distinction between the individual's involvement in mysticism and the conscious intellectual relating of this experience with the structure of the religious system to which the mystic is committed. We must recognize the basic structure of the latter to interpret the actual expression and interpretation given to his experience by the mystic. At the same time with regard to the mystical experience as an occurrence within the individuality of the mystic, we must recognize that *because of* the experience the conscious relating and evaluation takes place.

Two correlated dangers are relevant in this type of comparative study: oversimplification in the interpretation of the mystic's orientation within his religious structure, and distorting selectivity in determining the passages used to "represent" the mystical traditions. As to the first, there is no doubt that reducing any of the greater religions to a few pages of summary oversimplifies the system. Also, since the treatment in each case is designed to enable the Christian to attain a positive insight into the meaning of the system, certain aspects must receive an emphasis not always properly counter-balanced with other equally-present aspects. The general pattern followed in the simplification is designed to allow the mystics to be understood, and not necessarily the full implications of their religious structure. The principal safeguard against falsifying effects of simplification lies, therefore, in the fact that we are interested primarily in the mysticism of individuals within given religious structures and not in the structures as such or in the particular systematic characteristics of mysticism arising from specific religious traditions.

As to distorting selectivity in the choice, translation and arrangement of texts, again we are uninterested in whether or not the passages are "representative" of one or another religious tradition as such. We are interested in gaining insight into *mystics*. Since we must seek such insight from within the context of our own religious orientation, the significance of the mystical involvement of others for us depends on whether or not they are able to "speak" to us. The brief summary of the orientation of each tradition given at the beginning of the texts should counter-balance the selection distortion, at least with regard to possibly latent syncretism.

Finally, the range of mystical traditions represented should help to safeguard a basic objectivity as well as reveal the breadth actually involved in ecumenism. The traditions of Ancient Egypt and Zoroastrianism are two (from among others) of particular importance in the context of the formation and development of Judaism, and hence indirectly and mediately of Christianity. Classic Hinduism and Buddhism represent a tradition in civilization and religion most alien to the West, and hence of utmost importance in any attempt at a comparative study. Confucianism and Taoism together provide the ideal entry into the traditions of China, the paradoxical correlation of humanism and mysticism, a paradox of possibly great significance for the contemporary West.

Ancient Egypt

"I am Yesterday, Today and Tomorrow, (I have) the power to be born a second time, (I am the divine hidden soul who creates the gods). . . ." These words begin the LXIVth Chapter of the collection of sacred writings called the "Chapters of Coming Forth by Day," and known to us as the Book of the Dead. Regarded by the Egyptians as the oldest of these sacred texts, the chapter is ascribed to the period between the First and Sixth Dynasties (or roughly five thousand years ago) and testifies to their belief in man's immortality and ultimate participation in transcendence.

For Christians, Ancient Egypt usually evokes one of two images: the idolatrous enemy of Israel, or the barbaric and exotic kingdom that preceded the glorious Greek civilization of classic art, politics and philosophy in the ancient world. But the discovery of the real Egypt reveals the oldest of civilizations in the West, with a continuous cultural and religious life spanning more than three millennia—the first written literature; the explorers of eastern Africa; an empire from Libya to Mesopotamia; the first religious reformer known to history, King Ikhnaton. What should be most impressive to the Christian, however, was Egypt's dedication of life to the final sacred fulfillment of man—reflected negatively in the elaborate funerary cult, and positively in such writings as the text with which this section was begun.

The origins of Egyptian religion go back to the primitive agricultural cults which arose with the discovery and development of agriculture in the Nile valley fifteen to twenty thousand years ago. At the beginning of the historic period Egypt achieved political unity under the so-called Old Kingdom, with religious cults centered in several sacred cities. The basic religious form appears to be polytheistic and dominated by a solar cult. Yet distinctions must be made. It is entirely possible that the Egyptian pantheon even at the earliest period implies a singular supreme Deity with associated superhuman beings created by him.* Thus, we read in the Hymn to the Sun that was recited each morning, "For you are the one who soars over the gods (and) there is no other god who soars over you." (The "divine hidden Soul who creates the gods" of the first cited text could be another example of this implication.) The archaic solar deity and father of all the gods was Ra, personified in the early period especially as Horus, the hawk-symbol of the sun at the height of the day-sky. Throughout all the dynastic era Ra remained the ultimate form of Divinity, although he might assume varied aspects and names, and be united to names from other cults as in the Theban *Amen-Ra*. When Ikhnaton attempted his full monotheistic reform, he chose the name *Aten* ("sun disk") to represent the Only Lord, yet retained the designation *Ra* to indicate the concept *divinity*.

* In archaic times each settlement had its singular god, conceived of completely within the context of the tribal grouping and without reference to the fact that the other settlements had their own "singular" gods. Egyptian unification brought these deities and their cultic centers together politically yet not theologically. Various attempts to resolve theological multiplicity were made, usually in terms of establishing the dominance of one cult form at the expense of the others. Monotheistic implications of this situation are obvious in the solution of the theological school of Memphis, which exalted the singularity of the city's god Ptah and reduced "other gods" to hypostases of Ptah; thus Ptah created the world through his voice, *Thoth* was his tongue, *Atum* was his thought, *Horus* was his heart, and so on.

A characteristic of Egyptian theological thought was the use of multiple names and forms to represent one idea. Thus Ra is identified by many names and given diverse characteristics all ranged side by side without any feeling of contradiction. Egyptian deities are constantly pictured by combining seemingly unrelated elements—human bodies, animal heads, parts of inanimate objects, etc. Relationships of parent-offspring given mythologically are often reversed without warning. Thus, Ra may be spoken of as creator of the sky goddess in one breath, and in the next be represented as her offspring. Many aspects of divinities seem grossly anthropomorphic, yet the Egyptians clung to them throughout all their history even while developing more sophisticated modes of expressing these abstractions. The conclusion that must be drawn is twofold: the Egyptians were reluctant to discard traditions of the past, and also (possibly *because* of this conservatism) sought to express abstract unity in diversity. Their thinkers were certainly aware of the necessities of rudimentary logic and so we must presume that the apparent contradictions so often found in their literature reflect compound ideation. (A unique exegetical section in the Book of the Dead, Cap. XVII, provides us with evidence for the presumption; a series of interpretive questions and answers is applied to a much older text, clearly demonstrating that the ancient theologians sought different levels of meaning in the multiple layers of the writings.)

The strongest proof that the theologians, at least, were monotheistic (in contrast to the folk-level of the popular religion) lies in the reform of Ikhnaton, with its clear monotheism. Many have held that Ikhnaton's reform bursts upon the scene as the unique product of a great mind breaking completely with the past. In reality it seems to be a true reform rather than a revolution. Recent studies have brought to light indication of a growing conflict between the monarchy and cultic priesthoods, especially that of the powerful Theban *Amen-Ra*. Ikhnaton (1375–1358 B.C.) with his undoubted theological interest and insight, comes at the end of a developing struggle reaching back to the Thuthmosid monarchs.* But apart from this politico-religious history, we have evidence of a theological recognition of the unicity of divinity in the implications of many of the most venerable non-Ikhnaton texts (such as the *Hymn to Ra* from the Book of the Dead presented here). The Ikhnaton reform attempted to purify an already existing tradition from the outmoded archaisms and the confusing use of compound ideation. The force behind the reform was the intense vision of Ikhnaton. The reform failed not because Egypt was not ready for monotheism but because of the opposition of the established cult priesthoods together with the polytheistic beliefs of the masses.

* An interesting correlation of materials tracing the development of antagonism between the monarchy and the priesthood of the state cult of Amen-Ra is given by Christiane Desroches-Noblecourt, *Tutankhamen* (New York: New York Graphic Society, 1963), pp. 34–36. The XVIII Dynasty Pharaoh Tuthmosis III planned to have an obelisk erected in the precincts of the great Temple of Amen. But the stone memorial was dedicated to the Sun (as personified by *Harmakhis*), not to the supposedly supreme Amen. Although completed, the obelisk was not erected until the reign of Tuthmosis IV, grandson of Tuthmosis III. Erecting this obelisk at Karnak, and another to Harmakhis at the great Sphinx, Tuthmosis IV was denying that he owed his elevation to the throne to the powerful Amen. However, at the death of his father Amenophis II, during a procession in the Temple of Amen the priests carrying the statue of the god unexpectedly brought the image to Tuthmosis (not his father's heir) and thereby pretended that Amen himself had miraculously chosen the new king. Tuthmosis' symbolic acts of reverence for Harmakhis (and against Amen) are indicative of the growing resistance of the monarchy against clerical domination by the Amenite priests. It is Amenophis IV—better known as Ikhnaton—who follows the policies of his grandfather Tuthmosis IV to their theologically logical conclusion: the Solar-symbolized monotheistic reform. (The original "anti-clerical" obelisk of Tuthmosis III now stands before the Cathedral of St. John Lateran in Rome.)

The earliest Egyptian beliefs of immortality presumed a bodily resurrection from the grave. This was superseded by an immortality conceived of as a perfected life in a glorious paradise beyond the grave, where all earthly pleasures and occupations would continue. The final development was more abstract and conceived of man as eternally present with the divinity, accompanying Ra in the solar ship as it crossed the heavens ceaselessly. In the sacred texts we find both the paradise notion and the idea of eternal presence maintained side by side.

But there is the additional teaching that man somehow becomes divine. By divine decree man becomes one with the Only One in a real and mystic act of unity. The Book of the Dead tells us that this act of unity is achieved through supplication and the possession of revealed sacred wisdom through which the deceased will know how to identify himself with Osiris, the principle of divine life and immortality and mythic ruler of the dead. Throughout the texts the deceased is made to speak as if he were the Divinity. He uses Osiris' name for his own. He assumes to himself all the prerogatives and attributes of the Divine.

For Ikhnaton mystic identity is conceived of as sonship:

You are in my heart and no other knows you
But your Son, Ikhnaton, whom you have enlightened
To understand your might and designs.

Under the symbolism of the sun—*Ra* and *Aten*—we see some of the principal characteristics of the suprahuman as known by the Egyptians: light, benevolence, power, source of fertility, majesty, infinity, eternity, paternity, and beauty. The idea of God as Beauty points to a recognition of the divinity as essentially spiritual although usually approached in terms of con-

crete personifications and images. Divine Beauty recurs again
and again in the sacred literature and finds its apex in the
Ikhnaton texts and in his constant use of the mystical liturgical
exclamation, "How beautiful Thou art!"

HYMN TO RA*

ADORATION

A Hymn of Praise to Ra
when He rises in the eastern part of heaven.
Those who are in his train rejoice,
and behold, Osiris Ani the victorious says:
Hail, O Sun-disk,
O Lord of Rays,
who rise on the horizon day by day!
Shine with your beams of light
upon the face of Osiris Ani
who is victorious,
for he sings hymns of praise to you at dawn,
and he makes you to set at evening
with words of adoration.

* The *Hymn to Ra* is drawn from the Theban Recension of the Book of
the Dead (Chapter XV). The version presented here follows closely the translation given by E. A. Wallis Budge, *The Book of the Dead* (London: Rout-
ledge and Kegan Paul, 1949), Vol. I, pp. 71–78.
    The *Hymn to the Sun* is attributed to King Ikhnaton; for other translations,
the reader is directed to Mayer and Prideaux, *Never to Die* (New York:
Viking Press, 1938), pp. 162–165, and A. Erman, *The Literature of the
Ancient Egyptians* (New York: E. P. Dutton, 1927), pp. 289–291.
    Both texts and much of the introductory material of this section appeared
originally in the author's article "Immortality and Transcendence," *International Philosophical Quarterly* (December, 1962).

May the soul of Osiris Ani,
the triumphant,
come forth with you into heaven,
may he go forth in the Matet Boat.
May he come into port in the Sektet Boat,
and may he cleave his path
among the never-resting stars in the heavens.

Osiris Ani, being in peace and in triumph,
adores his Lord,
the Lord of eternity, saying:
Homage to you, O Heru-khuti,
who are the god Kherpera,
the self-created,
when you rise on the horizon
and shed your beams of light
upon the lands of the North and of the South,
you are beautiful,
yes beautiful,
and all the gods rejoice
when they behold you,
the King of heaven.

The goddess Nebt-Unnut is established upon your head
and her uraei of the South and of the North
are upon your brow;
she takes up her place before you.
The god Thoth is placed in the bows of your boat
to destroy utterly all your foes.
Those who are in the Tuat
come forth to meet you,

and they bow in homage
as they come towards you,
to behold your beautiful Image.

And I have come before you
that I may be with you
to behold your Disk every day.
May I not be shut up in the tomb,
may I not be turned back,
may the limbs of my body be made new again
when I view your beauties,
as those of your favored ones are,
because I am one with those who worshipped you
while alive on earth.
May I come to the land of eternity,
may I come even to the everlasting land,
for behold, O my Lord,
this you have ordained for me.

MYSTERY

And behold, Osiris Ani triumphant in peace,
the triumphant one, says:
Homage to you,
O you who rise in your horizon as Ra,
you rest upon order
which does not change nor can be altered.
You pass over the sky,
and every face watches you and your course,
for you have been hidden from their gaze.

You show yourself
at dawn and at evening day by day.
The Sektet Boat, in which is your Majesty,
goes forth with might.
Your beams shine on all faces;
the number of your red and yellow rays cannot be known,
nor can your bright beams be depicted.
The lands of the gods
and the eastern lands of Punt (Somalia)
must be seen before they can be described,
and before that which is hidden in you may be measured.
Alone and by yourself
you manifested yourself
when you came into being above the sky.

May Ani advance
just as you advanced;
may he never cease to go forward,
just as your Majesty does not cease to go forward,
even though it be for a moment;
for with strides in one little moment
you pass over the spaces
which would require hundreds of thousands and millions
   of years
for a man to pass over;
this you do and then sink to rest.
You put an end to the hours of the night
and you count them, even you.
You end them in your own appointed season,
and the earth becomes light.
You set yourself before your handiwork

in the likeness of Ra,
and you rise in the horizon.

THEOPHANY

Osiris, the scribe Ani, victorious,
declares his praise of you when you shine,
and when you rise at dawn
he cries in his joy at your birth:
You are crowned with the majesty of your beauties;
you mould your limbs as you advance,
and you bring them forth without birth-pangs
in the form of Ra,
as you rise up into the upper air.
Grant that I may come
to the heaven that is everlasting,
and to the mountain
where your favored ones dwell.
May I be joined to those shining beings,
holy and perfect,
who are in the next world,
and may I come forth with them
to behold your beauties
when you shine at evening
and go to your mother, the night sky.
You place yourself in the west,
and my two hands are raised in adoration
when you set as a living being.
Behold, you are the maker of eternity
and you are adored when you set in the heavens.
I have given my heart to you without wavering,
O you who are mightier than the gods!

EVER-CREATOR

Osiris Ani, the triumphant, says:
A hymn of praise to you,
O you who rise like gold
and who flood the world with light
on the day of your birth.
Your mother gives you birth upon her hand,
and you give light to the course of the Sun-disk.
O you great Light who shine in the heavens,
you strengthen the generations of men with the Nile-flood
and you cause gladness in all lands,
and in all cities,
and in all the temples.

You are glorious because of your splendors,
and you make strong your *ka*
with *hu* and *tchefau* foods,
O you who are the mighty one of victories,
you who are the Power of all Powers,
you who make strong your throne against evil fiends;
who are glorious in majesty in the Sektet Boat,
and who are exceedingly mighty in the Atet Boat,
make Osiris Ani glorious
with victory in the next world;
grant that in the netherworld he may be without evil.
I pray you to put away his faults behind you:
grant that he may be one of your venerable servants
who are with the shining ones;
may he be joined to the souls
which are in Tatchesertet
and may he journey into the field of lilies

by a prosperous and happy decree,
he the Osiris, the scribe, Ani the triumphant.

UNITY

And the god replies:
You shall come forth into heaven,
you shall pass over the sky,
you shall be joined to the starry deities.
Praise shall be offered to you in your solar boat,
you shall be hymned in the Atet Boat;
you shall behold Ra in his shrine,
you shall set together with his Disk day by day,
you shall see the Ant fish when it springs into being
in the waters of turquoise,
and you shall see the Abtu fish in its hour.
It shall come to pass that the Evil One shall fall
when he lays a snare to destroy you
and the joints of his neck and of his back
shall be hacked asunder.

Ra sails with a fair wind,
and the Boat draws on and comes into port.
The mariners of Ra rejoice,
and the heart of Isis is glad,
for (Death) the enemy of her lord has fallen to the ground.
You shall behold Horus
on the standing place of the pilot of the boat,
and Thoth and Maat (wisdom and truth)
shall stand one on each side of him.
All the gods shall rejoice

when they behold Ra coming in peace
to make the hearts of the shining ones to live,
and Osiris Ani, victorious
scribe of the divine offerings of the lord of Thebes,
shall be along with them!

HYMN TO THE SUN

UNIVERSALITY

You arise beautiful on the horizon of heaven,
O living Sun-Disk, who first ordains life!
You rise in the eastern horizon
And fill every land with your beauty.
You are beautiful and great and shining
And are high above every land.
Your rays encompass the lands
Even to the bounds of all you have created.
You are Ra and reach to every land
And unite them all for your beloved Son.
You are afar off, but your rays are upon the earth,
You are before man's face in your coming and going.

When you go down in the western horizon
The earth is in darkness like death,
Men sleep in their chambers with covered heads
And no eye can see another.
The things under their heads might be stolen
Yet they would not know it.
The lion comes forth from his den and serpents bite,

There is the Dark and the earth is in Silence,
For he who creates rests in his horizon.

When you rise at dawn and shine as Aten
You dispel the darkness.
The Two Lands awake rejoicing
And stand on their feet for you have awakened them.
They wash their bodies and take their garments
And raise their arms adoring your rising.
The whole land goes to its work,
The cattle rejoice in their pasture,
The trees and plants grow green,
The birds fly forth from their nests
And their wings give worship to your spirit.
All the wild beasts greet you with dancing,
All that fly come to life at your rising.
The ships sail upstream and down
And all ways are open because you arise.
The fish in the river leap up to your face
And your rays reach down into the sea.

CREATOR

Creator of seed in men,
Creator of issue in women,
You give life to the son in the womb of his mother,
And soothe him that he may not weep,
O nurse in the womb.
You give life-breath to all you create.
When the child comes forth on the day of birth
You open his mouth and provide what he needs.

When the chick in the egg cries out in the shell
You give it the strength to break forth,
And it comes forth from the egg to chirp
And walks on its two legs!
Your works are vast and hidden from us,
Sole God to whom no other is likened!
You alone made the earth
Fashioning all that go upon legs and fly with wings.
You created the lands of Syria and Ethiopia and Egypt,
You put each man in his place and supply his needs.
Each one has his provision and his lifetime is reckoned.
You determine the speech of their tongues
And distinguish the forms of their bodies,
For you distinguish all land and all peoples.
You create the Nile in the Underworld
And bring it forth to sustain mankind.
You have made men for yourself,
The Lord of them all, weary on their behalf,
The Lord of all lands, rising for them,
The Sun of the day, Almighty!
You make all the far lands to live,
And for them you have made a Nile in the sky
That it may rain down for them
Making streams on the hills like the sea
To give water to the fields of their towns.
How perfect are your counsels, O Lord of Eternity!
The Nile in the sky is made for foreign lands
And for all the wild beasts that walk upon feet,
While the Nile from the Underworld comes forth for Egypt.
Your rays nourish all the fields
And they grow when you shine down.

You have made seasons to sustain them,
The winter to cool, the summer to warm.
For yourself you have made a heaven to rise in,
There to behold all you have made below.
You are alone, appearing in form as the Living Sun
Creating millions of forms from yourself,
The cities and towns, the fields, roads and rivers,
All eyes see you radiant before them
As you shine as the Disk of the day.

REVEALER

You are in my heart and no other knows you
But your Son, Ikhnaton, whom you have enlightened
To understand your might and designs.
The earth came into being when you raised your hand,
When you rise men live, when you set they die.
You yourself are Lifetime and men live in you.
All eyes look upon your beauty until you set,
All work is finished when you go down in the West.
When you rise again the work of the King goes forward
For you have placed all men on the earth for your Son,
The Lord of Diadems, King of the Two Lands,
Who lives on Truth, Ikhnaton, Son of Ra,
And for the great royal consort whom he loves,
The mistress of the Two Lands, Nefretete,
Who lives and is young forever.

Zoroastrianism

In the years immediately preceding the explosion of the Persian conquerors into the Neo-Babylonian Empire and the world of the Greek city states, the prophet Zoroaster (dates disputed: c. 660–583, or? c. 570–500 B.C.) undertook a radical reform of the primitive Persian nature religion. Besides establishing the basis of a world religion which dominated the Near East for more than a thousand years, Zoroaster's central doctrine of dualism between good and evil has had influence on other major religious traditions, including Judaism, Mediterranean gnosticism and Christianity. The mainstream of orthodox Christianity has struggled against dualist influence since the Apostolic period (as evidenced, for example, in some of the condemnations of the First Johannine Letter), during the Manichaean challenge exemplified by Augustine's career, in the Neo-Manichaeism of the Middle Ages and in the seemingly indestructible puritanism introduced by Jansenism. It is ironic that the influence of Zoroaster's teaching should continue to be felt among Christians and Christian-influenced Western society, in spite of the irreconcilable structures of Christianity and Zoroastrianism.

It is also ironic that the divisiveness of dualism should be the dominant effect of Zoroastrianism, an effect apparently not intended by the founder. In undertaking the reform of the Persian variant of the primitive Aryan nature cult, Zoroaster built upon two fundamental insights: Divinity was totally singular, not plural, and evil, whether physical or moral, cannot be the responsibility of the One All-Good God. He reduced the nature pantheon to the singular *Ahura Mazdah* (the Wise Lord) from whom eternally emanated the six *Amesha Spentas,* or personalized representations of abstract attributions: *Vohu Manah* (Good Mind), *Asha Vahihsta* (Highest Righteousness), *Khshathra Vairya* (Divine Dominion), *Spenta Armaiti* (Holy Devotion), *Haurvatat* (Salvation) and *Ameretat* (Immortality). Opposed to the Wise Lord in his emanations was *Ahriman,* the principle of evil, who was also found multiple through a host of evil spirits—most of whom can be identified mythologically with the older gods of the primitive Aryans. Mysteriously, *Ahriman* is independent in existence but destined to be definitively defeated by *Ahura Mazdah* at the end of time.

Zoroaster conceived of cosmic history as divided into four periods, each three thousand years in duration. At the beginning only spirit existed, the creation (or emanation) of the Wise Lord, himself a pure spirit. *Ahriman,* however, produced matter, and in the conflict between *Ahura Mazdah* and *Ahriman* matter and spirit became mixed, forming the basis for the conflict of good-and-evil, light-and-darkness, that Zoroaster saw as characteristic of historical existence. The third period of the world was that in which the faith of Zoroaster would be propagated, preparing the way for the eschatological struggle of the future savior, *Saoshyant,* at whose triumph Evil would be forever conquered, the matter of the universe annihilated, the believers would rise from the dead and the everlasting kingdom of Spirit would be inaugurated. Those who had rejected the message of Zoroaster would fall into a fiery hell as they attempted to pass over *Chinvato Peretav,* the Bridge of the Separator, at a Last Judgment.

The coexistence and independence of *Ahura Mazdah* and *Ahriman* represent a thoughtful theological attempt to remove the problem of evil from the Godhead, conceived of as Absolute Good. The identification of a separate and ultimate source of evil unfortunately entails two major problems, apparently not clearly realized by Zoroaster. First, granted that an independent principle of evil effectively removes the problem of evil originating from a Good God, this dualism inescapably gives rise to an even more difficult metaphysical problem: how can the Good God be Absolute in any ultimate sense in the presence of the co-eternal and definitively independent *Ahriman*? It seems that Zoroaster was content to resolve this problem with the doctrine of the eventual irreversible conquest of *Ahriman* by the Wise Lord. Yet all later Zoroastrian-descent dualists have recognized and attempted solutions for the apparent metaphysical contradiction of "two infinites."

The second problem raised by this type of dualism is the necessity to repudiate one or more areas of our perception of existence. It is inevitable that the opposing principle of evil be concretized—otherwise it could not be of significance in the religious commitment of the individual. And what we term "evil" is first known within specified phenomenal contexts, especially so-called physical evil. Sickness, pain and death and natural catastrophies being found in the context of the material or tangible "stuff" of our existence, a tendency towards a dualistic structuring of reality almost necessarily must result in the identification of matter with evil.* But, as a result, the individual

---

* It is interesting to note that this pattern of matter-spirit antagonistic dualism occurs in cultures which have been under the influence of Persian culture—immediately or mediately—but is missing in non-influenced cultures. Thus, the Near East, Mediterranean and European-American peoples tend to be negatively dualistic: the divisions matter-spirit, male-female, etc., always suggest tension or incompatibility between the two elements. Of all Western peoples the Semites seem least involved in this tendency, yet traces of it can be found in post-Babylonian Judaism and Islam. In marked contrast to this pattern, the Far East, Negro Africa and pre-Columbian America seem totally untainted. Thus, for Confucius the division male-female can suggest nothing but complementarity and harmony.

must logically repudiate the very basis of phenomenal knowledge. Thus, he faces a double contradiction: matter must be ultimately unreal, although this judgment is in response to a need to explain the reality of historic evil within the context of matter; life to continue must be supported on matter, yet the acceptance of such support must be some sort of commitment to evil. From Zoroaster to the contemporary folk-Jansenist these contradictions have given rise to a religious schizophrenia. The world is ripped into two opposed spheres; the individual's inescapable involvement in material reality must always be "reconciled" with his ideological spiritual exclusiveness; there is a pathological guilt in pleasure and enthusiasm in pain; there must be an "excuse" for life itself.

But for Zoroaster, the prophet and mystic, the vision of the Wise Lord overshadowed such issues. And we must judge his quest for unity in God in terms of the subjective positiveness of his thought. If his dualism is the basis for subtle and far-reaching difficulties, it is also the subjective basis for an individual's unreserved commitment to the mystic Presence as the Infinite Good—Goodness Itself, the Good for all mankind, making individual existence noble, outgoing and significant.

GATHAS*

DEDICATION

The Dominion is yours and the power for deeds!
Protect your poor, O Wise One with Right and Good Mind!

* The present translation of these selections from the *Gathas* follows, in most instances, the Duchesne-Guillemin translation's order with its division of lines. For the most recent edition of the entire text, cf. Jacques Duchesne-Guillemin, *The Hymns of Zarathustra* (London: John Murray, Ltd., 1952).

Uniting ourselves with you we renounce all evil things:
False gods and faithless men.

Since you actually are thus, O Wise One with Right and
   Good Mind,
Grant me this sign: the remaking of existence
So that with greater joy
I may approach you in worship and praise.

(Yasna XXXIV: 5, 6)

REVELATION

With hands stretched out in prayer for support,
O Wise One with Righteousness, I will ask of you
The acts of the Holy Spirit,
That I may satisfy the will of Good Mind . . .

To me who worship you, O Wise Lord with Good Mind,
I ask according to Righteousness that you give success
In both worlds—that of body and that of mind—
Supporting me through them and bestowing bliss.

To me who would sing your praise as never before,
As Righteousness, O Good Mind and Wise Lord,
And to them for whom Devotion increases that Dominion shall
   not decrease,
Come at my call and give me support.

Fulfill the desire of the pure whom you have found worthy,
For their Righteousness and their Good Mind,
O Wise Lord, let them attain it!

I know that words of prayer that are good are effective before
you.

You who guard Righteousness and Good Mind,
Teach me, O Wise Lord, to proclaim your revelation
According to your spirit as if through your own mouth,
How the beginning of existence happened.

(*Yasna* XXVII: 1, 2, 3, 10, 11)

DIVINE DESTINY

May the Wise Lord who rules at will
Grant to each one of us whatever he desires!
I desire to have strength and perpetuity
To maintain Righteousness—grant me this, O Devotion—
The rich rewards, the life of the Good Mind.

May the Supreme Good be ours—
As one desires may he receive heavenly joy
Through your all-revealing Spirit, O Lord,
The mysteries of the Good Mind which you will give as
    Righteousness,
With joy of long life all days!

O Wise Lord, I recognized you as the Holy One,
When I saw you at the beginning, at the birth of life,
Establish a recompense for deeds and words:
Evil to the evil and good to the good,
Through your wisdom at the last crisis of creation.

(*Yasna* XLIII: 1, 2, 5)

ELECTION

O Wise Lord, I recognized you as the Holy One
When as Good Mind he came to me and asked:
Who are you, whose are you?
Shall I appoint the days by a sign
When judgment shall be made about your substance and
    yourself?

O Wise Lord, I recognized you as the Holy One
When as Good Mind he came to me.
To his question: To whom will you give worship?
I answered: While I offer my adoration to your fire
I will fix my mind upon the Right with all my might.

O Wise Lord, I recognized you as the Holy One
When as Good Mind he came to me,
When I was first instructed in your words.
Will my zeal in carrying out what you told me
Is the greatest good cause suffering among men?

O Wise Lord, I recognized you as the Holy One
When as Good Mind he came to me
To learn the compass of my desire:
Grant me this—to know that which ensures
Long duration of desired existence which is in your Dominion.

O Wise Lord, I recognized you as the Holy One
When as Good Mind he came to me and said:
The Silent Thought inspired me to proclaim the greatest good.

Let no one favor those of Evil
For they are the enemies of the Righteous.

(Yasna XLIII: 7, 9, 11, 13, 15)

UNIFICATION

He who first filled space with light through Mind,
Who through his will created Righteousness,
Whereby he maintains the Good Mind—
You have increased this, O Wise One, by your Spirit
Which is one with you, O Lord!

O Wise One, through mind I have known you
As the first and last, as father of Good Mind,
When with my eyes I beheld you as the creator of
    Righteousness,
The Lord in the deeds of life!

From the fullness of his own communion with Integrity and
    Immortality,
And with Righteousness and Dominion,
The Wise Lord shall make lord of Good Mind
Him who is his friend in spirit and deed.

The insightful man understands clearly:
He who knows Righteousness through Good Mind as
    Dominion,
He helps him in word and deed.
O Wise Lord, he shall be your most devoted companion.

(Yasna XXXI: 7, 8, 21, 22)

Hinduism

The religious history of India spans more than three millennia, is rooted in the fusion of diverse peoples and cultures, and embraces literally hundreds of distinct schools, cults and sects. Yet this most pluralistic of all Eastern societies is also characterized by an extraordinary degree of organic wholeness in religion. This paradox arises from the fundamental Indian vision of Reality: the seemingly infinite number of things is only an illusion; there is but one Real, God.

To understand this commitment to pure monism and something of its implications, we must recognize the formative effect of the three major stages of earlier Indian religion. Corresponding with the Aryan invasion and conquest, and the subsequent development of the rigid caste system, the first stage of development extends over a period of nearly two thousand years and is marked by the composition and compilation of the sacred literature known as the *Vedas*. The semi-nomadic Aryans came down into northern India, conquering the great prehistoric agricultural civilizations of the rich river basins, and bringing with them their religion of sky-gods. As further west in Iran and Mediterranean Europe, the conquerors' sky-gods and the earth-fertility-gods of the native civilization gradually merged into a single religious system which, in turn, gave rise to the sacred traditions of mythology, ritual and lore recorded in the Vedic writings. But unlike the other Aryan-dominated societies of the West, the new Indian civilization gave rise to the rigid caste system which immobilized social class. The caste system certainly owes part of its origin to the fact that the Aryan conquerors were vastly outnumbered by the native peoples and hence sought to preserve their identity and socio-political position by making permanent the conqueror-conquered relationship in terms of heredity. But as in all pre-modern societies, with no distinction drawn between "religious" and "secular" values, the caste system quickly became the foundation of the fused religion.

By the first millennium before Christ the Vedic period of development came to an end and the main lines of the socio-religious system were set. Within this context the first schools of Indian philosophy emerged, producing the next major corpus of speculative writings, the *Upanishads*. By approximately 600 B.C., certain principal philosophical structures have been established that will determine all future development of Indian thought. First, there arose the conviction of the continuity of life through reincarnation after death. Although not the only factor in this development (since such notions are not uncommon in more primitive societies), the fact of the rigidity of the caste system certainly played a major role in making reincarnation a permanent doctrine of Hinduism. The injustices of hereditary caste—for the masses poverty, servitude, sickness, early death, and for the privileged few wealth, despotism and irresponsibility to any human law—generated a profound pessimism towards the value of the historic present but also an ultimate optimism towards the possibility of a reversal of injustice in a future condition. In the Upanishadic period this hope for the future was concretized in the concept of reincarnation, whereby the good of this life would find reward in the achievement of a suitably superior life in the future, whereas the evil would be reborn in appropriate degredation. It must be noted that the reincarnation doctrine is not simply "believed," it is taken as self-evidently true, and all Indian life takes place consciously within its context. Implied in such an acceptance of reincarnation is a realization of the impermanence and valuelessness of anything here-and-now. Although at first one might presume that permanence and value will be found in a future reincarnated state, Upanishadic philosophy recognized that inextricably bound up with reincarnation was the realization of the transitoriness of everything pertaining to life. Thus, there arose the conviction of the total absence of reality in everything that appears to exist. This second fundamental doctrine of Hinduist metaphysics may be simply stated: the infinite number of things appearing to exist simply do not exist, all things, including the mind and consciousness of the knower, are illusion. To the question, what causes this massive illusion? classic Hinduism answered: Brahman—the Godhead—the only Reality. Hence, coupled with the doctrines of reincarnation and phenomenal illusion is the doctrine of pure monism.

The popularization of Upanishadic philosophy took place in the last few centuries before Christ. During this third foundational period two occurrences of immediate interest to us take place: the formation of Buddhism by Gotama (to be considered in the next section) and the composition of the *Bhagavad-Gita*, or "Song of the Lord." Written as a dialogue between Arjuna (a legendary warrior-hero) and Krishna (Brahman appearing in human guise), the *Gita* was destined to become the most important single work of the Hindu sacred literature. With rare exceptions, nearly every school, cult and sect of Hinduism since the third century before Christ draws upon the *Gita* and regards it as normative for the essence of Hindu religious tradition. Although the *Gita* is found inserted within the text of the *Mahabharata*, an immense epic poem of one hundred thousand verses, it is actually an independent composition and is usually treated as such.

It is a treatise on man's relationship to God, illusion to Reality. As a forceful exposition of Hinduist monism it attempts to give a positive and meaningful answer to the problem raised by embracing Brahman as the only Real. (In our present consideration we should realize that theistic monism is not pantheism. The latter holds that all the things of the universe in themselves and together constitute Divinity; monism holds that there is literally nothing—no things, no universe—only Divinity.) The *Gita* teaches that man and the universe he seems to live in are unreal. God alone is real. Why do the illusions occur? God —the Unmanifest—manifests Himself. Thus, the illusoriness of things is this: they seem to be these various things, but they are not—their self-identity is the illusion; their "true self" is actually God. In the illusion that there is something, God paradoxically manifests the Only, God. The *Gita* draws out the implication for man in this doctrine: the individual must realize that he is not truly himself, that there is ultimately only one true-self, God, therefore man annihilates the illusion of false-self by recognizing what it is (or, rather, is not), by rejecting the illusion of reality in himself and in all other seeming beings, and by embracing the only true self, God.

Putting aside the intellectual commitment to such a metaphysics, it is clear that theistic monism requires mysticism to occupy a central place in the life of man. Through realization the individual conceives of his unity with God as a oneness *in se* (a fusion, absorption or identification, rather than a union of one with the other). Obviously realization of the Presence is the only fact of significance possible in life. Psychologically the monist mystic has one great advantage in that rational "knowledge" of the Presence through *concept* is of no significance—everything as illusion can be nothing more than a *sign*, illusion not reflecting the nature of Reality but paradoxically symbolizing it by negation as the non-illusion.

In spite of the profound difference in metaphysical commitment between monist Hinduism and non-monist Christianity, the Hinduist experience of the mystical state as evidenced in the passages drawn from the *Bhagavad-Gita* has obvious relevance to that of Christians. Again, we must distinguish between the conscious intellectual interpretation given to the mystical state by any individual—necessarily reflecting doctrinal commitments—and the structural elements we are able to discern in mysticism as a human-suprahuman process. Thus, whether or not the human is an illusion, this is a human experience of the attempt to realize oneness with the suprahuman. Hence, the Christian and Hinduist mystics somehow meet in the experience of God, speak of it so that each knows the other as a participant in that oneness, yet also speak of it so that each is separated by the differences between their visions of Truth.

BHAGAVAD-GITA*

THE ABSOLUTE

One looks upon It as a wonder,
another speaks of It as a wonder,
another hears of It as a wonder,
and even after having heard of It,
no one really does know It.

(Chapter II)

* The selections from the *Bhagavad-Gita* are based on the translation of Kashinath Trimbak Telang, *The Sacred Books of the East*, Vol. VIII (New York: Charles Scribner's Sons, 1900). Cf. also Prabhavananda and Isherwood, *The Song of God: Bhagavad-Gita* (New York: New American Library, Mentor Edition, 1954).

WORSHIP

Brahman is the oblation,
with Brahman it is offered up,
Brahman is in the sacrificial fire,
and by Brahman it is cast in,
and Brahman, too, is the goal
to which he proceeds
who mediates on Brahman in the action.

(Chapter IV)

DETACHMENT

He who knows Brahman,
whose mind is steady,
who is not deluded,
and who rests in Brahman,
does not exult on finding anything agreeable
nor does he grieve on finding anything disagreeable.
One whose self is not attached to external objects,
obtains the happiness that is in the self,
and through concentration of mind,
joining one's self with the Brahman,
one obtains indestructible happiness ...
The worshipper whose happiness is within,
whose recreation is within
and whose light also is within,
obtains divine bliss
becoming one with the Brahman ...
He attains tranquility,
knowing me to be the enjoyer

of all sacrifices and penances,
the Great Lord of all worlds
and the friend of all beings.

(Chapter V)

DIVINE LIFE

The highest happiness comes to such a worshipper
whose mind is fully tranquil,
in whom the quality of passion has been suppressed,
who is free from sin
and who is become one with the Brahman.
Thus constantly devoting his self to abstraction,
a worshipper freed from sin
easily obtains that supreme happiness:
assimilation with the Brahman.
He who has devoted his self to abstraction,
by devotion looking alike on everything,
sees the self abiding in all beings,
and all beings in the self.
To him who sees me in everything,
and everything in me,
I am never lost
and he is not lost to me.
The worshipper who worships me
abiding in all beings,
holding that all is one,
lives in me
however he may be living.

(Chapter VI)

... the ancient Seer, the ruler,
more minute than the minutest atom,
the supporter of all,
who is of an unthinkable form,
whose brilliance is like that of the sun,
and who is beyond darkness ...

(Chapter VIII)

THE SUPREME MYSTERY

Now I will speak to you ...
of that most mysterious knowledge,
accompanied by experience,
by knowing which you will be released from evil.
It is the chief among the sciences,
the chief among the mysteries.
It is the best means of sanctification.
It is imperishable,
not opposed to the sacred law.
It is to be apprehended directly
and is easy to practice ...
those who have no faith in this holy doctrine
return to the path of this mortal world
without attaining to me.

This whole universe is pervaded by me
in an unperceived form.
All entities live in me
but I do not live in them ...
As the great all-present atmosphere
always remains in space,
know that similarly all entities live in me.

But the high-souled ones
who are inclined to godlike nature,
knowing me as the inexhaustible source of all,
worship me with minds not turned elsewhere.
Constantly glorifying me
and exerting themselves, firm in their vows,
and saluting me with reverence
they worship me always devoted.
All others offering up the sacrifice of knowledge
worship me as one, as distinct
and as all-pervading in numerous forms.

(Chapter IX)

THE SUPREME DESTINY

The wise, full of love, worship me
believing that I am the origin of all
and that all moves on through me.
Placing their minds on me,
offering their lives to me,
instructing each other and speaking about me
they are always contented and happy.
To these who are constantly devoted
and who worship with love
I give that knowledge by which they attain to me.
And remaining in their hearts,
I destroy with the brilliant lamp of knowledge
the darkness born of ignorance in such men only
out of compassion for them.

You are the supreme Brahman,
the supreme goal,

the holiest of the holy . . .
You only know yourself by yourself.
O best of beings, Creator of all, Lord of all,
God of gods, Lord of the Universe!

(Chapter X)

VISION

And, O Lord of the universe,
O you of all forms!
I do not see your end or middle or beginning.
I see you bearing a crown and mace and disk—
a mass of glory,
brilliant on all sides,
difficult to look upon
having on all sides the effulgence
of a blazing fire or sun,
and indefinable.
You are indestructible,
the supreme One to be known.
You are the highest support of the universe.
You are the inexhaustible protector of everlasting piety.
I believe you to be the Eternal Being.
I see you void of beginning, middle, end—
of infinite power,
of unnumbered arms,
having sun and moon for eyes,
a mouth like a blazing fire,
heating the universe with your radiance.
For this space between heaven and earth
and all quarters are pervaded by you alone.

Looking at this wonderful and terrible form of yours,
O high-souled One, the three worlds are fearful!

(Chapter XI)

UNION

Thus have I declared to you
the knowledge more mysterious
than any mystery.
Ponder over it thoroughly
and then act as you will.
Once more listen to my excellent words,
most mysterious of all.
Strongly do I like you
therefore I will declare what is for your welfare.
Place your mind on me,
become my worshipper,
sacrifice to me,
reverence me
and you will certainly come to me.
I declare to you truly,
you are dear to me.

(Chapter XVIII)

Buddhism

In the twenty-five centuries since his death, hundreds of millions of men from eastern Persia to Japan, from central Siberia to Indonesia, have come to venerate Siddhartha Gotama (c. 563–483 B.C.) as the Buddha, the Enlightened One. His doctrine with the Holy Order of those who embrace it has become, together with Christianity and Islam, one of the three most influential and widespread of the world's greater religions. In spite of its loss of western Asia to Islam, its virtual extinction in India, the land of its birth, its probable extinction in Communist Asia and the intellectual crisis it must face as the remaining Buddhist peoples of Asia undergo the cultural revolution of western science and technology, Buddhism today is still very much alive in its strangely "passive" and serene way and has the potentiality of great intellectual influence on the West, as yet hardly hinted at.

As Buddhism arose in the India of the sixth century before Christ, it rests axiomatically upon two of the three basic doctrines of ancient Hinduism: the continuity of life after death through rebirth and the illusory nature of the supposed reality of things. However, the peculiar insight of Gotama's genius proposed a metaphysics radically different from that which finds its classic expression in the *Bhagavad-Gita* two centuries later.

According to the traditions of the Buddha's life and teachings,

148

he was born the heir to the ruler of a small state at the present Indian-Nepalese border. His father, fearing he might give up his princely rank and seek enlightenment as a holy man, raised Gotama in worldly surroundings and kept him away from a knowledge of the human condition of suffering. Eventually, however, Gotama discovered the deception and was so deeply struck by the fact of man's sickness, old age and eventual death that he renounced his rank and took up the search for enlightenment. For several years he followed the traditional path of Hinduism, embracing the most rigorous forms of asceticism. However, after seven years of the severest austerities he came to the conclusion that such practices offered no hope of enlightenment. In this great turning point of his search, he began a meditation on the meaning of human existence and the fulfillment of that existence. In the course of that meditation he achieved the enlightenment he sought.

To understand something of the Buddha's insight and hence of all subsequent doctrinal development, we must view the basic issue in the light of his vantage point. As we have seen, the philosophy elaborated in the Upanishadic period was founded upon a basically pessimistic view of man's historic condition—the mass of mankind was demonstrably unhappy—and hence the fundamental philosophic task was one of finding a solution to the human problem. Gotama took the pessimistic evaluation for granted (quite logically), and also took for granted the first two steps in its solution—the world was illusion and life continued. (Westerners tend to be repelled by the pessimistic Indian starting point and overlook the genuine optimism implied in the seeking of a solution—whatever we may think of the solution.)

Orienting the entire issue of existence, human and cosmic, toward the problem of historic man, the Buddha realized what are termed the Four Holy Truths:

1. the very constitution of *everything* is *suffering.*
2. *suffering* depends upon *desire;*
3. the *annihilation of desire* is the *annihilation of suffering;*
4. this annihilation is possible through the practice of the Noble Eight-Fold Path (the series of eight progressive realizations of the illusion of *desire-suffering).*

With rigorous logic he rejected the notion that the illusion of existence was caused by the Godhead—recognizing that if *things* were *unreal,* then *unreal things* had *unreal causes,* which are *no causes at all.* Accepting axiomatically that existence was an illusion, the transposition of this abstraction into human terms meant that there is no substance, permanence or identity for man—*man is suffering.* Recognizing that the causality proposed in Hinduism was logically unreal, he boldly removed causality from metaphysics—illusion is a mere negation. Putting aside any subjective evaluation of this core of Buddhist teaching (whether or not it appeals psychologically, whether or not it is negative and pessimistic), two particularly religious questions arise quite naturally: Is Buddhism atheistic, and is Buddhism nihilistic? For apart from an interest in Buddhism as a system of religion, it would seem that an atheistic-nihilistic structure would preclude any consideration of Buddhist religious mysticism. Certainly the theoretical structure we have been using— human-suprahuman unity—would be meaningless without a human and suprahuman!

At the outset we must recognize that the Buddhist structure does not directly state: There is no God, man ceases to exist. If Buddhism is atheistic and nihilistic this can be no more than indirectly implied by the metaphysical structure. Removing the illusion of phenomenal reality from a divine causality is simply the logic of *something not causing nothing.* There is complete silence with regard to any *something*—Buddhism addresses itself only to the problem of the illusory *nothing*. The Buddha's contemporaries were involved in complex metaphysical theories about the nature of the Godhead (there were more than seventy competing theistic theories). The traditions record many instances of attempts to question Gotama on the subject. To all he gave the same reply: Do not occupy yourselves with such speculations. He expressed neither atheism nor agnosticism. His avoidance of the issue must be seen in terms of the epistemological implications of his metaphysics.

If everything is illusion (or, humanistically, suffering), then the total *knower, knowing* and *known* are simply unreal. Logically, then, no "real" can be spoken of since an analogy drawn from the "unreal" is a contradiction. One cannot say that a *something* is in any way like a *nothing*. Since our (unreal) experience is limited to nothing, the One Real is literally inconceivable and hence must be linguistically absent. Godhead and Reality, then, must not be found within Buddhism *as a system*, but they are necessarily implied within Buddhism *as a process*. The goal of the Buddha is not to annihilate reality, but to annihilate *unreality*, implying. . . .

Such implication, although always logically unspoken, is made most forcefully when Buddhism speaks of man at the conclusion of the process of the Noble Eight-Fold Path: *This totally illusory man is annihilated and therefore in the state of changelessness,* Nirvana. Such a statement is either a most unsophisticated self-contradiction or a purposeful linguistic contradiction, implying but logically never saying that there is something else about man—the opposite of illusion, of unreality—in a state of existence —the opposite of transitoriness, of non-being.

This structure of thought, so psychologically alien to most in the West, is designed to lead to "eloquent silence." The ultimate of man is indicated in his seeking. The ineffable is not conceived of, spoken of or named. Paradoxically because Buddhism sees man and cosmos as illusion, it sees that man and cosmos *must cease to be illusion.*

Therefore, as in the case of classic Hinduism, we recognize Buddhism as purely monistic in structure. But, again as with Hinduism, we can approach the central mysticism of Buddhism (whereby the unreality of illusion is realized) as distinguishable from the theoretical structure to which the mystic consciously and intellectually relates his experience of the mystical state.

But unlike Hinduism, Buddhist negative monism presents its mysticism in a peculiarly negative monist form. Thus, evaluation by the Westerner is a difficult task, in constant danger of misinterpretation (both in seeing Buddhist and Christian statements as alike and as unlike!), with an unfortunate tendency towards a lack of psychological and emotional sympathy.

Noting the usually partly closed eyes of the figures of Buddhist sacred art, one Westerner concluded that Buddhism refuses to look at the world, is selfishly introspective and inhumanly passive. Yet in reality the Buddha looked very hard at the world to see behind or beyond its evident transitoriness; the Buddha taught altruistic compassion for the suffering of all things so that suffering might be eradicated; the Buddha journeyed back and forth across northern India for forty years after his enlightenment, preaching a message of ultimate hope to the helpless masses, denying the sacred validity of the caste system and urging a life of compassionate service to others as the prerequisite to personal perfection. For the Buddhist, the half-closed eyes are the sign of the serenity of enlightenment, when the inner eye has been opened,* not seeing with the mind but with union.

* Cf. Augustine: "Long for this Light . . . such as your bodily eyes do not know, a light to see for which the inward eye must be prepared." (*Enarrationes in Psalmos*, 41:2; used in the selections from Augustine, p. 70.)

WISDOM

What is Wisdom?
Wisdom is manifold and various,
and an answer that attempted to be exhaustive
would both fail of its purpose
and tend to still greater confusion.
Therefore we will confine ourselves to this meaning:
Wisdom is knowledge
consisting in insight
and conjoined with meritorious thoughts.

(Visuddhi-Magga, XIV)*

And what, O priests, is the discipline in elevated Wisdom?
Whenever, O priests, a priest knows the truth concerning
   misery,
knows the truth concerning the origin of misery,
knows the truth concerning the cessation of misery,
knows the truth concerning the Path
leading to the cessation of misery,
this, O priests, is called the discipline in elevated Wisdom.

(Anguttara-Nikaya, III:88)

DELIVERANCE

He who considers (the constituents of being)
in the light of their transitoriness

* The selections from the *Visuddhi-Magga* and the *Anguttara-Nikaya* are
taken from Henry Clarke Warren, *Buddhism in Translation* (Cambridge:
Harvard University Press, 1947). The selections from the *Fa-Kheu-King-Tsu*
are adapted from Samuel Beal, *Texts from the Buddhist Canon* (London:
Trubner and Co., 1878). (This is about to be reissued.) A translation of the
Heart Sutra, with introductory notes, is given in Edward Conze, *Buddhist
Scriptures* (London: Penguin Books, Ltd., 1959).

abounds in faith and obtains the unconditioned deliverance;
he who considers them
in the light of their misery
abounds in tranquility and obtains the desireless deliverance;
he who considers them
in the light of their lack of inner self
abounds in knowledge and obtains the empty deliverance.

(*Visuddhi-Magga,* XXI)

THE NOBLE PATH

Here the unconditioned deliverance is the Noble Path
realized by meditation on Nirvana (Changelessness)
in its unconditioned aspect.
For the Noble Path is unconditioned
from having sprung out of the unconditioned,
and it is a deliverance
from being free from the corruptions.
In the same way the Noble Path
when realized by meditation on Nirvana (Changelessness)
in its desireless aspect
is to be understood as desireless;
when realized by meditation on Nirvana (Changelessness)
in its empty aspect
as empty.

(*Visuddhi-Magga,* XXI)

ILLUMINATION

The disciple who is able to hold the precepts firmly;
like a wall, difficult to be overturned,
he surrounds himself with the protection of the Law,

and thus persevering perfects himself in saving Wisdom.
The disciple, with his mind enlightened,
by this enlightenment adds yet to his store of Wisdom
and so obtains perfect insight into the mysteries of Truth,
and thus illumined he practices the duties of his calling in
peace.
The disciple able to cast away sorrow
enjoys happiness in perfect tranquility,
and by virtuously preaching the Law of Eternal Life,
himself obtains Nirvana (Changelessness).
By hearing he acquaints himself
with the Rules of a Holy Life;
he shakes off doubt and becomes settled in faith.
By hearing he is able to resist
all that is contrary to the Law (Truth),
and so advancing, he arrives at the place
where there is no more Death.

(Fa-Kheu-King-Tsu, III)

FAITH

Faith can cross the flood,
even as the master of the ship (sails across);
ever advancing in the conquest of sorrow,
Wisdom lands us on the Other Shore.
The wise man who lives by faith,
in virtue of his holy life enjoys unselfish bliss,
and casts off all shackles.
Faith lays hold of true Wisdom;
Religion leads to deliverance from Death;

from hearing comes knowledge,
which brings with it enlightenment;
faith with obedience is the path of Wisdom:
firmly persevering, a man finds escape from pain,
and is thus able to pass over
and escape the gulf of destruction.

(Fa-Kheu-King-Tsu, IV)

THREE TREASURES

The man who takes refuge in the Enlightened One,
this is the man who obtains real advantage.
Therefore, night and day he ought ever to reflect on
the Enlightened One, the Law and the Brotherhood.
Thus reflecting continually on the Three Treasures,
and on impermanency and on himself,
reflecting on moral duty and on compassion,
on the emptiness of all things around him,
and their unreality:
these are subjects for contemplation.

(Fa-Kheu-King-Tsu, VI)

LOVE

If a man lives a hundred years
and engages the whole of his time and attention
in religious offerings to the gods,
sacrificing elephants and horses and other things,
all is not equal to one act of pure love in saving life.

(Fa-Kheu-King-Tsu, VII)

MANUAL
OF THE HEART (SECRET)
OF THE PERFECTION
OF THE WISDOM
OF THE OTHER SHORE

THE UNREALITY

There are the five elements-of-existence,
void in their very nature . . .
Here form is emptiness,
and emptiness indeed is form.
Emptiness is not different from form,
form is not different from emptiness . . .
All things bear the characteristic marks of emptiness.
They do not come into being,
they do not cease to be:
they are not stainless,
they are not stained;
they do not become imperfect,
they do not become perfect.
Therefore here in this emptiness there is no form,
there are no sensations, notions or mental propensities;
there is no consciousness;
there is no eye, ear, nose, tongue, body or mind;
no color, sound, odor, taste or object of touch;
no constituent element of vision or other sense processes,
no constituent element of the mental processes.
There is no knowledge, no nescience,

no destruction of knowledge, no destruction of nescience . . .
There is no destruction of old age and death;
there is neither any coming into existence
nor any ceasing of suffering;
there is no path to the destruction of suffering.
There is no enlightenment,
no attainment,
no realization
since enlightenment does not exist.

THE ENLIGHTENMENT

There are no obstacles of thought
for the (one) who cleaves
to the Wisdom of the Other Shore.
Because there are no obstacles of thought,
he has no fear;
he has transcended all wrong notions;
he abides in enduring Nirvana (Changelessness).
All the Enlightened Ones of the past, present and future,
cleaving to the Wisdom of the Other Shore,
have awakened to the highest, perfect, complete awakening.
Therefore one should know
the Wisdom of the Other Shore
is the great mystic formula,
the mystic formula of great wisdom,
the most excellent mystic formula,
the peerless mystic formula,
capable of allaying every suffering.
It is truth because it is not falsehood.

A mystic formula has been given
in the Wisdom of the Other Shore.

It sounds as follows:
O YOU WHO ARE GONE, WHO ARE GONE,
WHO ARE GONE TO THE OTHER SHORE,
WHO HAVE LANDED ON THE OTHER SHORE:
O YOU ENLIGHTENMENT, HAIL!

.Confucianism

China of the sixth century before Christ, like India, was involved in an intellectual ferment of far-reaching consequences for the development of civilization. At this period in which India produced the towering genius of Gotama, classic China gave birth to Kung Fu-tzu, better known to the West as Confucius (c. 551–479 B.C.). Like the Buddha, Master Kung was to originate and dominate an intellectual and religious tradition of massive importance for twenty-five centuries. Yet here the resemblance between these men, their teachings and civilizations apparently ends.

The China of Confucius was a welter of feudal states nominally owing allegiance to the last degenerate successors of the great Chou Dynasty who ruled what was by then an empire in name only. The gradual disintegration of imperial authority and the consequent rise of feudal absolutism marked a corresponding decline in public and private morality, scholarship and the arts, and overall political and economic stability. The society of feudal China was divided into three principal classes: the hereditary nobility, their ministers, warriors and civil servants, and the artisans, workers and peasants. Most of the members of the feudal "middle class" of socio-political functionaries were from families in some way remotely related to the ruling nobility, but usually economically depressed. Confucius was born into such a family and grew to manhood under the shadow of poverty. He was endowed with an eager mind and, in spite of his limited means, worked himself into the ranks of the civil service of his feudal state. As time went on and he saw more and more of the evils of his degenerate society—war, oppression of the poor, the decline of learning and the arts of civilization—he determined to devote himself to the salvation of his people.

Unlike his Indian contemporaries he determined to take man and the world as he found them and work for what he felt must be a restoration of a previous lost stage of perfection. Through the classical writings and traditions of the pre-feudal Chou Dynasty and the supposedly earlier legendary dynasties, he attempted to reconstruct an ideal order of civilization in which the true nobility would be those who followed and preached this Way of Harmony, taught and served by the scholar-politicians who devoted themselves to the study and execution of the ultimate Principle of Truth behind mankind and the cosmos. For Confucius the world about him was real, dynamic, perfectible and ultimately sacred.

In the middle of his life Confucius took up the role of the teacher of the Way. As a teacher he insisted on ability in his students rather than nobility or weath, taking as disciples many from the poorest families.* He sought to raise up a band of scholarly followers who would carry his teachings to all of China, and at the same time he hoped to be appointed prime minister in one of the states so that he could put his teaching

---

* Confucius' attitude concerning the extension of learning outside the feudal limits of social and economic class was quite radical. Thus in Book VII, Chapter 7, of the *Analects* we read:

The Master said: From the poorest upwards, from the man who could bring no better offering than a bundle of dried meat, not one has ever come to me without receiving instruction.

into practice. As the designer of state policies based on the Way, he sought to convince the feudal rulers by concrete example of the validity of his teaching. Although he succeeded fully in founding a school of disciples who carried his teachings throughout China and remade Chinese civilization into a Confucian civilization, he never achieved his ambition to begin the socio-political phase of restoration himself.

Many commentators on Confucianism find it difficult to recognize it as a religious system, especially since later Neo-Confucianism is clearly a non-theistic humanism. It is true that Confucius concentrates all his attention on culture, the arts, politics and morality, yet it is also clear that he saw these as human-cosmic reflections of an Ultimate. His emphasis is on man and his world—because these he can know directly and these constitute the dynamic Real here-and-now. Confucius has no interest in speculative abstration, isolated introspection or mythological escapism. He lives in a real world with real problems—all somehow meaningful in an ultimate sense.

First of all, he sees man in three dimensions: the *individual* who knows and acts, *society* as the counterpart to individuation and the absolutely necessary context of human existence, and the *cosmos* as the place of man's existence and the embodiment of the harmonious laws governing all things. There is no such thing as man alienated from the cosmos. All of phenomenal reality is integrated into an organic and dynamic whole. This integration is the sacred Harmony of Heaven (Heaven being the traditional Chinese symbol designating the Transcendent, the Divinity), and this Harmony is to be found manifested phenomenally in the laws of the cosmos, in the interrelation of men in society, and in the conduct of the individual as he responds to the dynamics of living. Although Confucius is absolutely opposed to any form of individualism that would call into question man's socio-cosmic nature, he recognized that mankind's participation in the ultimate Harmony of Heaven depends exclusively on the individual man—he must act, he must learn, he must be responsible.

The key to Confucianism, therefore, is to be found in two central themes: *Li* and *Jen*. If man acts in this universal dynamics, he must act in specific ways, he must do *this* or *that*. *Li* means "ritual," embracing the total modality of human activities. Ritual includes the sacred rites of religion, the ceremonies of the familial veneration of ancestors (not worshipping them, but expressing the continuity of society regardless of time and individual death), the forms of courtesy and social intercourse, and literally every action of man from scholarship and the arts to everyday speech and work. For Confucius, then, human activity is profoundly meaningful and is the medium reflecting what Heaven is as well as giving access to the Transcendent. Hence it is essential that man study and know the norms of moral conduct, ceremonial, forms of courtesty, the arts and the traditions of the archetypal past. It is also essential that man lives *li*.

Confucianism is often called the "religion of *li*," but it is also the way of *jen*. It is impossible to translate *jen* directly. The Chinese written character for *jen* is composed of the symbol for "man" and the symbol for "two," intended to indicate something proper to the social dimension of man. *Jen* embraces a wide range of meaning. It includes moral goodness, whereby social intercourse is possible; it extends to the ability to act as a human in accord with the order of nature; it includes the inner potential to perceive and pursue truth, beauty, artistic discipline and creativity. In short, *jen* is the mysterious basis for all genuinely human response to reality, specifically to reality mediated to man by *li*. *Jen* is also the mysterious dynamism of the Transcendent, and when perceived as such is the Absolute to man.

The core of Confucianism can be expressed systematically in the following structure:

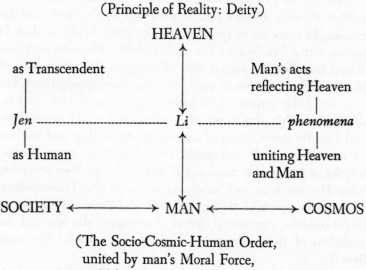

(Principle of Reality: Deity)

HEAVEN

as Transcendent | Man's acts reflecting Heaven

Jen ---------- *Li* ---------- *phenomena*

as Human | uniting Heaven and Man

SOCIETY ⟷ MAN ⟷ COSMOS

(The Socio-Cosmic-Human Order,
united by man's Moral Force,
or *Te*)

The usual difficulties most Westerners have in seeing Confucianism as a religion properly so called rather than as a system of ceremonialism, politics and secularist moralism must be focused in an irreducible paradox: for Confucius the "secular" as we encounter it is actually the manifestation of the sacred; hence for Confucius the proper pursuit of the so-called secular constitutes the supreme function of religion.

This brings us to the problem of mysticism in Confucianism. Put quite simply, is there any? Certainly what we might regard as the "usual" notion of mysticism has no place in the religion of *li*—and Confucius himself specifically denied that he was endowed with insight or knowledge beyond the rational.* Yet an understanding of the core of Confucianism seems to insist that we regard this vision of reality and man's pursuit of it as within the essential structure of mysticism. Confucianism is totally committed to the unity of the human and suprahuman. It calls for man to see within the apparently shallow world of appearances the ultimate and absolute Presence. And this is not simply to be understood, it must be *lived* so that man, cosmos and transcendent Heaven are unified in fulfilling Harmony.

GREAT LEARNING†

THE WAY

What the Great Learning teaches is:
to manifest illustrious virtue,
to renew the people,

---

* "The Master said: I myself am not one with innate knowledge; I am simply one who loves the past and is diligent in studying it." *Analects*, Book VII, Chapter 19.

† The *text* of the *Great Learning* is ascribed to Confucius himself, as is the case with the *text* of another of the Confucian classics, the *Doctrine of the Middle Way* (the *commentary* sections, however, are certainly of much later date). The selections from the *Analects* are from those portions of the work believed to date from the generation immediately following the death of the Master. Hence, together with the *text* of the *Great Learning* we are dealing with the oldest level of Confucian thought before the development of the later interpretive schools and before the fundamental reinterpretation made by Mencius. The translations have been made from the Chinese texts of James Legge, *The Chinese Classics*, Vol. I (Oxford, 1893), and generally follow his translations; however, many modifications have been introduced in the *Analects* passages following Arthur Waley, *The Analects of Confucius* (London: George Allen and Unwin, Ltd., 1938).

and to rest in the highest excellence.
The point where to rest being known,
the object of pursuit is then determined,
and, that being determined,
a calm unperturbedness may be attained.
To that calmness there will succeed tranquil repose.
In that repose there may be careful deliberation,
and that deliberation will be followed by attainment.

THE ORDER

Things have their root and their branches.
Affairs have their end and their beginning.
To know what is first and what is last
will lead near to what is taught in the Great Learning.

ATTAINMENT

The ancients who wished to manifest illustrious virtue
throughout the kingdom first ordered well their own states.
Wishing to order well their states,
they first regulated their families.
Wishing to regulate their families,
they first cultivated their persons.
Wishing to cultivate their persons,
they first rectified their hearts.
Wishing to rectify their hearts,
they first sought to be sincere in their thoughts.
Wishing to be sincere in their thoughts,
they first extended to the utmost their knowledge.

Such extension of knowledge
lay in the investigation of things.
Things being investigated,
knowledge became complete.
Their knowledge being complete,
their thoughts were sincere.
Their thoughts being sincere,
their hearts were then rectified.
Their hearts being rectified,
their persons were cultivated.
Their persons being cultivated,
their families were regulated.
Their families being regulated,
their states were rightly governed.
Their states being rightly governed,
the whole kingdom was made tranquil and happy.

THE ROOT

From the Son of Heaven to the mass of the people,
all must consider the cultivation of the person
the root of everything.
It cannot be when the root is neglected
that what should spring from it
will be well ordered.
It never has been the case
that what was of great importance
has been slightly cared for,
and also that what was of slight importance
has been greatly cared for.

ANALECTS

MYSTERY

Some one asked the meaning of the Great Sacrifice.
The Master said: I do not know.
Anyone who knew its meaning
could deal with all that is under Heaven
as easily as he could look at this
(and he pointed to the palm of his hand).

(Book III: 11)

KNOWN AND UNKNOWN

Tzu-kung said: We are permitted to hear
the Master's views on culture
and the manifestations of the Good (Transcendent).
But he will not speak to us at all
on the nature of man
and the Way of Heaven.

(Book V: 12)

COMMITMENT

The Master said: They who know the Truth
are not equal to those who love it,
and they who love it
are not equal to those who delight in it.

(Book VI: 18)

PARTICIPATION

The Master said: Great indeed was Yao as sovereign!
How sublime was he!
There is no greatness like that of Heaven,
and only Yao corresponded to it.
How vast was his virtue!
The people could find no name for it . . .

(Book VIII: 19)

THE ABSOLUTE

(Speaking of the Transcendent Good) Yen Hui sighed:
The more I gaze upwards to see it
the higher it seems to go,
the deeper I bore down into it
the harder it seems to become,
I look for it before me
and suddenly it seems to be behind.*
The Master skillfully leads men on in order:
He enlarged me with learning,
he taught me the restraint of ritual.
Even if I wished to stop I could not.
Having exerted all my ability,
Something seems to stand right up before me,
yet though I long to pursue it
I can find no way to it.

(Book IX: 10)

---

* For a striking parallel of expression, cf. Bernard of Clairvaux, *Sermons on the Canticle of Canticles*, 74:5 (this passage is given under the title "The Search" on p. 83). This text from the *Analects* is probably the most impressive evidence for the presence of a dimension of mysticism in the structure of Confucianism, independent of the relative absence of individual confucianists as mystics (in the sense of those involved in the mystical experience of interior consciousness). For a Taoist counterpart to this text, cf. pp. 174–175.

Taoism

Of all the greater religions of antiquity, Taoism is most directly oriented towards the involvement in the mystical process. In fact, it is not an oversimplification to say that Taoism is a system of mysticism.

The roots of Taoism go back into the prehistoric formative period of Chinese civilization, bound up with the mystic dualism of *Yin-Yang* as the bipolar principle of phenomenal existence. The most ancient statement of *Yin-Yang* doctrine is contained within the mystic divination system of the I *Ching*, or Book of Changes, one of the archetypal classics of China. The written text of the I *Ching* was known to Confucius, who, together with subsequent scholars, modified and edited the version that has come down to us. However, the work itself in its earlier oral form is at least a thousand years older. The Book of Changes presents a mystic model of the universe and all phenomena through a system of binary symbols, composed of broken lines (– –) representing the negative and solid lines (——) representing the positive in nature. The symbols are arranged in combinations of six such positives and/or negatives, forming hexagrams, thus:

and so on in sixty-four possible forms. Each hexagram is interpreted to symbolize a different aspect of reality according to the suggestiveness of positives-negatives. Although the system might appear naïve, especially when used for divination, it is actually a remarkable yet simple use of a binary mathematical model.* But what is important for the development of Taoism is the dualism of *Yin-Yang*.

Yin-Yang doctrine views all things accordingly to a universally applied analysis of reality into a positive (*Yang*) and a negative (*Yin*) category—thus for example, in man and animals, male and female; in qualities, strong and weak, active and passive; in physical states, dynamic and static, large and small. It is important to note, however, that *Yin-Yang* dualism differs radically from Zoroastrian-influenced dualistic systems in that it is in no sense distorted by the evaluative dualism of good-and-evil, spirit-and-matter, real-and-unreal. *Yang* as positive, active and male and *Yin* as negative, passive and female do not oppose each other, they are integrally complementary. Each differs, but the union of the differences constitutes the necessary wholeness —male is meaningless without the female. *Yin* and *Yang* are not in tension but in harmony.

Taoism pursues the ultimate unity implied in this dualistic harmony. It seeks the absolute Principle—symbolized by *Tao*, the "Way"—which stands, transcendent, behind the *Yin-Yang* dualistic manifestation of its Reality. In terms of man Taoism interprets the mystical process as a paradox of a reversal of values: what appears as strength is actually weakness, passivity

---

* The process of conceptualizing phenomenal reality in terms of a binary mathematical model is identical as a process with the model concept of the modern computer. The basic difference between the *I Ching* theory and the theory structure of the computer is one of relative complexity.

For the best presentation of the *I Ching* in English, cf. Richard Wilhelm, tr., *The I Ching or Book of Changes*, Bollingen Series XIX (New York: Pantheon Books, Inc., 1950). (This edition has an insightful and provocative introduction by Carl Jung.) For an excellent commentary on the *I Ching* for Westerners, cf., Hellmut Wilhelm, *Change*, Bollingen Series LXII (New York: Pantheon Books, Inc., 1963).

is actually activity. It is in the realization of this paradox in an interior intuition that mystical unity in the Absolute is achieved. Hence, Taoism may remind the Westerner of Christian quietism. Such a resemblance, however, is perhaps merely superficial. For seventeenth-century quietism is subtly influenced by the seemingly ever-present good-and-evil dualism of theological manichaeism: man abject, corrupt and powerless and hence totally passive in the confrontation of irresistibly dynamic grace. This is not the receptivity of Taoist mystics, which resembles more the simple openness and expectancy of Christian mystics such as Bernard of Clairvaux or John of the Cross waiting upon the transforming presence of the Lover. Perhaps the most illuminating instances of this Taoist state of subjective receptivity are to be found in such classic symbols as the power of water and the usefulness of a bowl. Taoism never tires of pointing to the apparent lowliness of water, always flowing down to the furthest crevices in the earth and the smallest cracks in rocks while the sun's heat and the blowing wind seem to dominate the world; yet earth and rocks are split apart with the irresistible force of water when it freezes. And if we ask, what constitutes the usefulness of a bowl? we realize that it is not in its solid sides and bottom but in the interior emptiness waiting to be filled. In each instance Taoism is not concerned with actual passivity, inaction or impotence but with the paradox that the apparent negative is actually the positive of reality, intensely active and powerful.

The history of the development of Taoism as a religious system reflects this central concern with the paradox of mystical reversal. For, except for a popular derivative form of magic and superstitious folk-religion, Taoism was not destined to continue long as a religion. Yet, paradoxically, it has had an important and lasting influence on Chinese and Japanese culture—epitomized in the magnificent tradition of ethereal landscape painting—and, more important still, on the formation of Chinese and

Japanese Ch'en, or Zen, Buddhism which absorbed this oldest of Chinese mystical systems.

Taoism seems to have fulfilled itself by disappearing! And its strange history is caught in the closing lines of the selection from the *Classic of the Pivot of Jade*:

But having attained to this (the Way)
you may forget all bodily form;
you may forget your personality;
you may forget that you are forgetting!

TAO TE CHING*

THE UNKNOWN

The Tao (Way) that can be trodden
is not the enduring and unchanging Tao.
The name that can be named
is not the enduring and unchanging Name.
Conceived of as having no name,
it is the Originator of Heaven and Earth.
Conceived of as having a name,
it is the Mother of all things ...

(Chapter I)

* The *Tao Te Ching*, a compilation of mystic poems, is the most important of the Taoist classics, and is ascribed to the semi-legendary Lao-Tzu, supposedly an elder contemporary of Confucius. The selections from the *Tao Te Ching* and from the *Classic of Purity* and the *Classic of the Pivot of Jade* follow closely the translations of James Legge, *The Texts of Taoism* (New York: Julian Press, 1959). Cf. also Arthur Waley, *The Way and Its Power* (New York: Grove Press, 1958).

THE GREAT MOTHER

There was something undefined and complete
coming into existence before Heaven and Earth.
How still it was and formless,
standing alone and changeless,
reaching everywhere and in no danger of being exhausted!
It may be regarded as the Mother of all things.
I do not know its name,
and I designate it the Tao.
Making an effort to give it a name
I call it The Great.
Great, it passes on in constant flow.
Passing on, it becomes remote.
Having become remote, it returns.
Therefore the Tao is great;
Heaven is great;
Earth is great;
the (Sage) King is also great.
In the universe there are four that are great,
and the (Sage) King is one of them.
Man takes his law from the Earth;
the Earth takes its law from Heaven;
Heaven takes its law from the Tao;
the law of the Tao is its being what it is.

(Chapter XXV)

THE ONE

We look at it
and we do not see it
and we name it "the Equable."

We listen to it
and we do not hear it
and we name it "the Inaudible."
We try to grasp it
and we do not get hold of it
and we name it "the Subtle."
With these three qualities
it cannot be made the subject of description,
and hence we blend them together
and obtain The One.
Its upper part is not bright,
and its lower part is not obscure.
Ceaseless in its action,
yet it cannot be named,
and then again it returns
and becomes nothing.
This is called the Form of the Formless,
and the Semblance of the Invisible;
this is called the Fleeting and Indeterminable.
We meet it and do not see its front;
we follow it and do not see its back.
When we can lay hold of the Tao of old
to direct the things of the present day,
and are able to know it
as it was of old in the beginning,
this is called discerning the clue of the Tao.

(Chapter XIV)

GREATEST AND LEAST

All-pervading is the Great Tao!
It may be found on the left and the right.

All things depend on it for their production,
which it gives to them,
not one refusing obedience to it.
When its work is accomplished,
it does not claim the name of having done it.
It clothes all things as with a garment,
and makes no assumption of being their Lord.
It may be named in the smallest things.
All things return to their root and disappear,
and do not know that it is it
which presides over their doing so.
It may be named in the greatest things.
Hence the sage is able to do his great works.
It is through his not making himself great
that he can accomplish them.

(Chapter XXXIV)

WISDOM

Without going outside his door,
one understands everything under the sky.
Without looking out from his window,
one sees the Tao of Heaven.
The farther one goes out from himself,
the less he knows.
Therefore the sages achieved their knowledge
without travelling,
gave their right names to things
without seeing them,
and accomplished their ends
without any purpose of doing so.

(Chapter XLVII)

CLASSIC OF PURITY

Now the spirit of man loves Purity,
but his mind disturbs it.
The mind of man loves stillness,
but his desires draw it away.
If he could always send his desires away
his mind of itself would become still.
Let his mind be made clean,
and his spirit of itself will become pure ...

(Chapter III)

In the condition of rest independently of place,
how can any desire arise?
And when no desire any longer arises,
there is the true stillness and rest ...
In such constant response and constant stillness
there is the constant Purity and Rest.
He who has this absolute Purity
enters gradually into the True Tao.
And having entered into it
he is called Possessor of the Tao.
Although called Possessor of the Tao,
in reality he does not think he possesses anything.
It is as accomplishing the transformation of all living things
that he is called Possessor of the Tao.
He who is able to understand this
may transmit to others the Sacred Tao.

(Chapter V)

CLASSIC OF THE PIVOT OF JADE

The Heaven-honored One says:
All you Heaven-honored men
who wish to be instructed about the Perfect Tao,
the Perfect Tao is very recondite
and by nothing else but itself can it be described.
Since you wish to hear about it,
you cannot do so by the hearing of the ear:
that which eludes both the ears and the eyes
is the True Tao;
what can be heard and seen perishes,
and only this survives.
There is much that you have not yet learned,
and especially you have not acquired this!
Till you have learned what ears do not hear,
how can the Tao be spoken of at all?   (Chapter I)

The Heaven-honored One says:
Sincerity is the first step towards the Tao.
It is by silence that that knowledge is maintained.
It is with gentleness that the Tao is employed.
The employment of sincerity looks like stupidity.
The employment of silence looks like incapacity.
The employment of gentleness looks like want of ability.
But having attained to this
you may forget all bodily form;
you may forget your personality;
you may forget that you are forgetting!   (Chapter II)

FIVE

Mysticism and Ecumenism

From the beginning Christianity has proclaimed itself the universal religion, revealed for the salvific fulfillment of all mankind. Although the ultimate significance of this universality necessarily remains inalterable as a metaphysical fact, this significance must be given conscious meaning within specific historical contexts. Emerging from within Judaism, earliest Christianity naturally enough conceived of universality in terms of Jewish hopes for the restoration of an earthly kingdom, extending this in the images of the celestial Jerusalem, a Neo-Davidic empire reaching to the ends of the earth and the calling of the nations under its sacral dominion. The de-Judaizing of Christianity begun by Paul and confirmed by the vigorous growth of Greek and Roman churches outside the synagogue demanded that universality be recast to embrace the classical world and especially its intellectual tradition. The early apologists began the process of "baptizing" the ancient philosophers who quickly contributed to Christian intellectual development, notably to the formation of systematized theology through such men as Augustine.

The destruction of the classical world, the invasion of barbarians from its narrowly-envisioned outer limits and the subsequent extension of Christianity among the new peoples throughout Europe necessitated a new conceptualization of Christian universality: Christendom. Sacred and civil society were coextensive; Western civilization was built upon a biblical image of the primordial past and a classical image of the world to be saved; beyond the edge of Europe was the indefinite fringe of lands of the surviving primitive pagans and the infidel Moslems. The destruction of the world-image of Christendom coincided with the age of discovery and colonial imperialism. The revelation of the real size of the world and its non-Christian population was met for the most part with a missionary imperialism calling for the direct overthrow and annihilation of non-Christian traditions. Though opposed by a few visionaries such as the great Ricci in China, conjoined civil and sacral colonialism dominated attitudes towards universalism for four centuries. And in the mid-twentieth century this conceptualization too is being swept away with the reassertion of the integrity of the peoples and cultures of Africa and Asia.

In spite of the example of the initial incorporation of Graeco-Roman tradition within Christian consciousness of its significance for all humanity, each stage of the conceptualization of universality has failed to form a theologically positive attitude towards the historical condition of the majority of mankind. True, individuals have been accounted for in terms of Christ— the serious will that all men be saved, the non-imputability of invincible ignorance. Although such notions provide a theoretical, theological basis for the salvation of the non-Christian, they can lead to peculiar conclusions—somehow non-Christians are indeed saved by Christ but not by Christianity, the revelation of Christ *for all men* never reaches beyond a small minority, more men are to be saved within an economy of ignorance than of active faith, and, most dangerous of all, one's religious way of life is a matter of practical indifference. These *can be* conclusions to be drawn from a non-positive attitude towards the historical condition of the majority of mankind. (They can be guarded against by rejecting them as false, but they always arise as objections to be answered.)

The general theological tendency has been to explain away non-Christianity rather than face it as a real part of the world in which Christianity has an ultimately fulfilling significance. If we are to attempt to develop, at last, a truly positive vision of Christian universality, one which meets the historic situation of the majority, we must build on a realistic appraisal of that situation. This is clearly demanded if there is any serious intent in extending the dynamism of inter-Christian ecumenism to non-Christianity. It is also demanded if Christians are to achieve a new awareness of universality in the new post-imperalist era.

Universality in terms of world population reveals that at present somewhat more than thirty per cent of mankind can be identified with one or another Christian body—but we are reminded that a large portion of this number represents purely nominal adherents and those without a genuinely personal commitment to Christianity as a way of life. If we project the present trends in population patterns and increase to the end of this century, we find that less than twenty per cent of the total world population will be in any way Christian. The missionary hopes of the last four centuries of Christianizing Africa and Asia are fading with the debacle of European colonialism. In addition, the condition of the Churches of the Americas forecasts serious erosion in the very areas where European expansionism has had permanent effect. (At this point mention should be made of the particular erosive force of the continuing conflict or tension between Christianity and so-called secularism. However, this aspect of the problem requires study outside the scope of the present inquiry.)

If we include in the population proportionality the dimension of the past, the question of universality becomes even more staggering. Until the last century we had no inkling of the actual age of the world and the human race. With rare and isolated exceptions, no people ancient or (relatively) modern presumed that human history extended back as much as ten millennia. Drawing from Hebrew conceptualizations, Christians traditionally envisaged all history before Christ as a period of little more than four millennia with a relatively small total population. We are now aware that human history stretches back well beyond a million years, and the total non-Christian population numbers in the billions. Thus, universality is not a question of how large a proportion of mankind the evangelizing effort of the Church can reach. Hence it seems that we must develop a new concept of universality, embracing this broader vision of man's extension in time and space.

One somewhat negative approach has been available for some time, namely to see universality as a two-part structure involving potential applicability on the one hand and actual receptivity on the other. It is argued that Christianity is always truly universal in the sense that as a way of conforming life to ultimate reality it can be meaningfully followed by any man anywhere and at any time. It is universally applicable. However, in the actual context of history not all men can receive the call to Christianity: those born before Christ, those not reached by the preaching of Christ, those who hear but are unable to respond. It cannot be universally received. While we can see a certain truth in this approach as coming to grips with one aspect of the historical situation, there is the grave danger of distorting the cosmic significance of Christ and the Church if we take this approach as a full answer. Without doubt, if Christianity is actually of universal significance then it must be applicable to any man (a truism), but this does not positively account for the historic *majority* who (apparently) are uninvolved in it. In other words, this approach merely says that Christianity *can be* universal, not that it *is historically*.

Many theologians seem to follow this approach, usually with one important correlate: although most *de facto* are not historically involved in the Church as such, all men somehow are involved in Christ as the actually universal savior. Whether they are aware of it or not, their ultimate destiny is achieved in terms of Christ. Those inculpably ignorant of Christ, His Work and His Church can be saved by living according to honestly formed conscience. Although historically not members of the Church, they are nonetheless not entirely outside the Church because of their necessary salvific relationship to Christ. This correlate is certainly realistic, it takes account of the universal significance of Christ and it stresses the ultimately universal effect of Christ and His Work. But does it face the problem of Christianity's universality? Is Christianity actually the way of life for all men? Or is the way for most men quite literally the *way of ignorance?* If such a suggestion is abhorrent to the Christian, then it seems that the development of another approach to universality is called for.

In the context of the multi-billion total population existing in a million and more years of history, Christianity should be seen in terms of the ultimate significance of Christ for all men and the significance of the actual ways of life men follow in the religious quest. These are the two concrete factors requiring our understanding. Perhaps we can find this understanding in our approach to the relationship of Christianity and Judaism. From the beginning Christians have recognized the organic unity of the Way of the Covenant of the Law with the Way of Christ. The Law was the preparation for Christ, whereby a people was drawn on historically to be able to receive the sought-for fulfillment; Christ was the fulfillment of the Law, the one for whom the preparation was made. Granted that Christ's significance extends beyond historic Israel (and hence that Israel's preparation itself must have a broader meaning), yet the irreducible relationship is Christ fulfilling Israel's quest. The most profound expression of this relationship is the compelling theme *in the fullness of time*: the moment of maturity, the completion of preparation, the quest achieved. Christ would be meaningless except at such a moment—meaningless to history, meaningless to Israel, meaningless to actual men awaiting the one who is to come. *Fullness of time*, thus, is twofold: the seekers and the sought.

Yet all men are seekers and, as Christians affirm, not in vain. Christ is their fulfillment whenever they live, however they seek. *Fullness of time*, therefore, must be a *fullness of times*, coming to one people after another in many ways at the completion of their preparation. For most their preparation reached fulfillment in the transhistorical Christ without awareness of the historical Christ. But with or without awareness, Christ is real, the fulfillment is real and the preparation is real. The many religious ways of life that have come from man are not meaningless in the face of Christianity. Without them there could be no *fullness of time* for each people either in the life of the individual or in the life of the community.

If Christ and His Church are inseparable, the Church somehow must be involved in Christ's fulfillment of all mankind. If Christ comes to man in the *fullness of times*, so does the Church. If Christ is actually universal, so is the Church. Christianity, the process of Christ-life, is integrally bound up in every way of life. This universal significance is positive for both Christian and Non-Christian. The Christian can perceive a meaningful continuity between whole ways of life and his own, rather than an atomizing of the human race and a repudiation of human effort. The Non-Christian is no longer the object of religious imperialism or paternalism, for the Christian can approach him as a brother serving his need to maintain continuity with the past.

Christianity would now be understood as actually embracing the entire human race, past, present and future—all seeking fulfillment in Christ, some with an awareness of Christ, but all involved. Those conscious of Christ are called to a ministry of service to their brothers, not conquest. The Church is a priesthood for the world, bearing Christ to the world.

This type of approach to universality entails neither syncretism nor indifferentism. Christianity does not seek to absorb other ways of life but to fulfill. Those elements genuinely preparatory to the fulfillment participate in the truth that is sought and hence have their historic validity in the life-process. Christianity is not in competition for man's allegiance—whether men realize it or not their religious expressions are Christian. It is not that any path man chooses leads equally to God, but that every path is ultimately the Christian path. The Christian task to the world, then, is to extend the awareness of Christ: not as if Christ is coming into the world as an alien, but that Christ is the one in whom all things already exist. The complete *fullness of time* for each religious community as a sacred tradition comes insofar as Christians succeed in awakening men to the Presence in whom they live. Christianity has successfully avoided both dangers of syncretism and indifferentism in its theological unity with Israel. There is no reason to expect the contrary as Christians realize their unity with all mankind. And this universal unity is unavoidable: Christ and the Church are one, dwelling one in the other, and Christ is come for all men. Historic divisions, unknowing and strife between Christian and Non-Christian are all too real. Historic distinctions, functions and structures within the Church are real. But an ultimate unity is also real if Christianity is actually of universal significance.

Appendix

Appendix

APPENDIX I

Islam: Sufist Mysticism

INTERIORIZATION

1. Religion of the heart. Sufism, a mystic tradition within Islam, stands opposed to two influences within Islam: worldliness that vitiates meaningful practice, and juridical formalism that vitiates interior spirituality on the part of the individual Believer. Against these extremes the Sufist tradition maintains that the paramount principle of religion is the love of God, and this is to be sought through asceticism and contemplation.

2. Approach. Sufism is not so much a sect as a way of initiation into traditional and metaphysical doctrine leading ultimately to spiritual realization in mysticism. To this end Sufism employs a number of methods: sacred poetry, music and dance, ritual recitation of litanies of the *Beautiful Names of God*, discipline for self-mastery, spiritual retreat and, most important, meditation.

3. Three-fold truth of Islam. Sufism views the revelation of God under three aspects:
   a. *shari'ah*: the exoteric law universally proclaimed;
   b. *tariqah*: the way of initiation leading to mystical spirituality;
   c. *haqiqah*: the spiritual reality achieved ultimately.

QUR'ANIC FOUNDATION

4. Mystic *ayah*. Sufists identify certain verses from the Qur'an as containing hidden mystical meaning which reveals itself in

meditation. These *ayah* are signs or proofs of the interior mystery of the presence of Allah. The core of Sufist mystical teaching is founded on the esoteric meaning (*batini*) contained primarily in these passages:

Wherever you turn yourselves to pray, there is the Face of God. (Q., 2:109)

Everything will perish except His Face. (Q., 28:88)

God encompasses them on every side. (Q., 75:20)

Say: God! And leave them to their vain amusements. (Q., 6:91)

This present life is only a toy. (Q., 62:19)

They do not make a proper estimation of God. (Q., 6:91)

I have chosen you for Myself. (Q., 20:43)

God knows, but you do not know. (Q., 3:59)

Be mindful of Me and I shall be mindful of you. (Q., 2:147)

If you love God, God shall love you. (Q., 3:29)

You will surely pass from state to state. (Q., 84:19)

Every soul will taste death, then you will return to Us. (Q., 29:57)

He creates and He restores to life. He is inclined to forgive and is gracious—the possessor of the glorious throne. (Q., 85:13–15)

You were dead and He gave you life. Hereafter He will cause you to die and again will restore you to life. Then you will return to Him. (Q., 2:26)

They shall meet their Lord, and they shall return to Him. (Q., 2:43)

We are God's and we shall surely return to Him. (Q., 2:151)

His is the kingdom of the heaven and the earth, and all things will return to God. (Q., 57:5)

It is to Him that you will return. (Q., 29:20)

Truly herein is an admonition to him who has a heart to understand, or gives ear and is present with an attentive mind. (Q., 1:36)

O you soul at rest, return to your Lord, well-pleased with Him, well-pleasing to Him. (Q., 89:27)

THE BEAUTIFUL NAMES OF GOD

5. Although there are several traditional lists of the Ninety-Nine Beautiful Names of God, the use of the Names as a ritual litany is fairly universal in Islam. "Rosaries" of ninety-nine beads (and complex finger-counting techniques) are employed, but without cult-object emphasis. The divine name *Allah* is called the *essential name* (*Ismu az-Zat*), while the Beautiful Names are the divine attributes. The theological concept of such mystic Names is derived from a reference in the Qur'an, 7:179. The following is the traditional list of Tirmidhi, as given by E. A. Wallis Budge, *Amulets and Talismans* (New Hyde Park: University Books, 1961), pp. 47–50.

1. The Merciful	15. The Dominant
2. The Compassionate	16. The Bestower
3. The King	17. The Provider
4. The Holy	18. The Opener
5. The Peace	19. The Knower
6. The Faithful	20. The Restrainer
7. The Protector	21. The Spreader
8. The Mighty	22. The Abaser
9. The Repairer	23. The Exalter
10. The Great	24. The Honorer
11. The Creator	25. The Destroyer
12. The Maker	26. The Hearer
13. The Fashioner	27. The Seer
14. The Forgiver	28. The Ruler

29. The Just
30. The Subtle
31. The Aware
32. The Clement
33. The Grand
34. The Forgiving
35. The Grateful
36. The Exalted
37. The Great
38. The Guardian
39. The Strengthener
40. The Reckoner
41. The Majestic
42. The Generous
43. The Watcher
44. The Approver
45. The Comprehensive
46. The Wise
47. The Loving
48. The Glorious
49. The Raiser
50. The Witness
51. The Truth
52. The Advocate
53. The Strong
54. The Firm
55. The Patron
56. The Laudable
57. The Counter
58. The Beginner
59. The Restorer
60. The Quickener
61. The Killer
62. The Living
63. The Subsisting
64. The Finder

65. The Glorious
66. The One
67. The Eternal
68. The Powerful
69. The Prevailing
70. The Bringer Forward
71. The Deferrer
72. The First
73. The Last
74. The Evident
75. The Hidden
76. The Governor
77. The Exalted
78. The Righteous
79. The Accepter of Repentance
80. The Avenger
81. The Pardoner
82. The Kind
83. The Ruler of the Kingdom
84. The Lord of Majesty and Liberality
85. The Equitable
86. The Collector
87. The Independent
88. The Enricher
89. The Giver
90. The Withholder
91. The Distresser
92. The Profiter
93. The Light
94. The Guide
95. The Incomparable
96. The Enduring
97. The Heir
98. The Director
99. The Patient

APPENDIX II

Consciousness and the Mystical Process

The following is a series of extracts from an article *Psycho-Chemistry and the Religious Consciousness* by Jean Houston, published by the *International Philosophical Quarterly* (September 1965). The question of the interrelation of the mystical process with the total consciousness process must include the full dimension of the human organism. It is unfortunate that the first publicized of the recent investigations into this area distorted the popular understanding of the scope and intent of empirical experiment and observation. Dr. Houston's investigations, although like all still only at the threshold, can give a valuable insight into some of the potentialities opening for us through the use of sound scientific methodology. In any attempt to correlate this aspect of study within the complex of mysticism, we should recognize the basic implication of the organic dimension: We cannot divorce mysticism from the mystic, and we must maintain the integrity of the mystic as a human. In other words: mystics are men, men have bodies, bodies are within the mystical process.

PSYCHO-CHEMISTRY
AND THE RELIGIOUS CONSCIOUSNESS

Since the time when man first came to the discovery that he was a foreconsciousness in a manifold world, he has sought to marshal the forces of analysis to control the manifold and perceive its natural laws. As a parallel movement to this analytic process there developed as an undercurrent another kind of gnosis: one that sought to discover man's essential nature and his true relationship to the creative forces behind the universe, and to discern wherein his fulfillment lay. For the sake of achieving this integral knowledge men have willingly submitted themselves to elaborate ascetic procedures and trained for years in yoga and meditation techniques. They have practiced fasting, flagellation and sensory deprivation, and, in so doing, may have attained to states of heightened mystical consciousness, but have also succeeded in altering their body chemistry. Recent physiological investigation into these practices in a laboratory setting tend to confirm the notion that askesis-provoked alteration in body chemistry and body rhythm is in no small way responsible for the dramatic change in consciousness attendant upon these practices. The askesis of fasting, for example, makes for vitamin and sugar deficiencies which acts to lower the efficiency of the cerebral reducing valve. The practice of flagellation will tend to release quantities of histamine, adrenalin, and the toxic decomposition products of protein—all of which will work to induce shock and hallucination.

The most comprehensive and consciously controlled system of disciplines is, of course, the Hatha Yoga which incorporates the practices of posture regulation, breathing exercises, and meditation. Its immediate aim is to bring under conscious control all physiological processes so that the body can function with maximum efficiency. Its ultimate aim is to arouse what is called *kundalini*, a universal vital energy which is supposed to gain access to the body at the base of the spine. When aroused and controlled, it is said to activate the psychic centers and thus make available to the yogi paranormal faculty. It is claimed that if this energy can be directed to the head center (the thousand petalled lotus) a mystical state is attained and the

yogi becomes aware of a mystical unitive consciousness. To this
end the early Sanskirt psychophysical researchers developed a
remarkable knowledge of physiological processes and their relation to body control. In their discovery of the *chakras* they
actually identified the endocrine glands. But what is more important, they realized that this series of glands, from the in-
terstitial, through the suprarenals, past the thymus, on past the
thyroid to the pituitary and culminating in the pineal, is a
sequence coordinated with and branching out from the spinal
cord. By developing techniques for the control of these glands
they sought to facilitate the raising of the spinal-based *kundalini.*

Extensive physiological testing of yogis now being conducted
in India and Japan would seem to indicate that these ascetics
are indeed capable of a remarkable degree of physiological control. This is particularly borne out in studies made with EKG
and EEG equipment, the yogis appearing to be able to exercise
control over frequency rhythms and voltage indicators.

Over twenty-five years ago in a volume entitled, *Poisons
Sacres, Ivresses Divines*, Philippe de Felice provided considerable documentation to support the age-old connection between
the occurrence of religious-type experiences and the eating of
certain vegetable substances. He wrote that the employment of
these substances for religious purposes is so extraordinarily widespread as to be "observed in every region of the earth, among
primitives no less than among those who have reached a high
pitch of civilization. We are therefore dealing not with ex-
ceptional facts, which might justifiably be overlooked, but with
a general and, in the widest sense of the word, a human phenomenon, the kind of phenomenon which cannot be disregarded
by anyone who is trying to discover what religion is, and what
are the deep needs which it must satisfy."

De Felice advanced the thesis that one of the earliest known
of these substances, the soma of the vedic hymns, may have

been indirectly responsible for the development of Hatha Yoga. The soma appears to have been a kind of creeping plant which the Aryan invaders of India brought down with them from Central Asia about 1000 B.C. The plant occupied an integral position in the myth and ritual structure of vedic religion, was regarded as divinity and was itself ritually consumed to bring the worshipper to a state of divine exhilaration and incarnation. "We have drunk soma and become immortal," hymns the early vedic author, "We have attained the light, the gods discovered." According to de Felice, as the Aryans moved deeper into India the gods proved more difficult to find as the soma plant would not travel. The exercises of the Hatha Yoga school, he suggests, may have been created as an attempt to fill the "somatic" gap and achieve that physiological state of being conducive to religious states of consciousness similar to those brought on by the ingestion of the sacred food. The larger implication of this thesis is that vegetable-provoked mysticism exists as a state prior to askesis-provoked mysticism: that early man may have come upon his first instances of consciousness change through his random eating of herbs and vegetables. Certainly this thesis can never move beyond the realm of conjecture although the fact remains that naturally occurring mind-changing substances are found the world over and are much more likely to have been experimented with before the creation of any system of mind-changing askesis.

The historic sacrality of the visionary vegetables has since given way to the modern notoriety of the synthetic derivatives —LSD-25, Psilocybin and Mescaline. One confronts these contemporary compounds with a host of puzzling questions. How may one reconcile the extremes of enthusiasm on the part of those who claim to find in these drugs the panacea for all ills with the vehement antagonism of those who are convinced that at best they mimic schizophrenia and at worst they work irreparable damage upon the brain? One is faced with the belligerent alternatives of whether these substances are mind-distorters or consciousness-expanders. (In Savage's phrase, do they provide "Instant Grace, Instant Insanity, or Instant Analysis"?) Finally, there is the tragic-cosmic denouement that these altercations have won for the drugs a pariah mystique. The problem with such a mystique is, of course, that it dictates that the pariah must go underground and fester in gnostic movements.

In an attempt to rescue psychedelic research from the Scylla of psychiatric a priorism and the Charybdis of gnostic transcendentalism, the *Foundation for Mind Research* initiated a program in LSD studies incorporating a variety of techniques and procedures. In this paper I shall discuss the results of one of these studies—the investigation of psycho-chemistry in its relationship to the religious consciousness. This study which involved almost 100 subjects was structured as an attempt to take depth soundings of the psyche and, in so doing, revealed a pattern of phenomenological descent. The pattern consisted of four levels: the sensory, the psychological or ontogenetic, the phylogenetic and the mysterium.

．　．　．　．　．　．　．　．　．　．

It remains to broach a tentative enquiry into the why and wherefore of phylogenetic awareness. Of course, one can only deal in the most theoretical of notions but perhaps the most likely explanation is to be had in a Jungian approach. I would suggest then along with Heinrich Zimmer that "ages and attitudes of man that are long gone by still survive in the deeper unconscious layers of our mind. The spiritual heritage of archaic man (the ritual and mythology that once visibly guided his conscious life) has vanished to a large extent from the surface of the tangible and conscious realm, yet survives and remains ever present in the subterranean layers of the unconscious. It is a part of our being that links us to a remote ancestry and constitutes our involuntary kinship with archaic man and with ancient civilizations and traditions."

Depth psychologists have pointed to the universality of psychic processes and the continuity of psyche within the race. We may add to this the theory that the psyche contains all the contents of time—extending backwards, across and through time; history being latently contained in each individual. It is my contention that the psychic depths and the time depths can be tested and explored through the medium of the guide in the psychedelic experience. The theoretical foundation for such a statement is that the ingestion of psychedelic substances evokes an activation of deeply buried psychic contents and a bringing of them to the surface of consciousness. As electrodes applied to memory or sensory areas of the brain can stimulate vivid and realistic recall at the moment of contact, so can suggestion activate phylogenetic memory in the subject undergoing the psychedelic experience.

There appears to be a real distinction between psycho-chemically evoked mystical consciousness and states of hypostatized sensory perception experienced as religious. The mystical state seems to represent the deepest strata in the subject's phenomenological experience, and, in most cases, is attained only after he has passed through a phylogenetic stage. It is then that the subject may cross the threshold into a mysterium experienced in almost every instance as the source level of reality. The semantics of theological discourse become visceral realities in the experiencing subject; the well known concepts referring to a "primordial essence" or an "ultimate ground of being" taking on an immediacy and directness hitherto unsuspected.

It is interesting to observe that those few subjects who descend to this level of mystical apprehension had in the course of their life demonstrated concern over questions of a religious nature. It would appear that where there is an intellectual predisposition and a willingness to acknowledge the phenomenon of religious and mystical experience, then such experience may more readily occur. Subjects of this type report a remarkable similarity in the structure and development of their experience. They often speak in terms of classic mystic and religious analogues. In almost every case the experience is initiated with a sense of the ego dissolving into boundless being. This process is almost always attended by an experience of the subject being caught up in a cascading preternatural light.

Another aspect of the experience is in the subject becoming aware of himself as continuous with the energy of the universe. It is frequently described with words to the effect that the subject was part of a dynamic continuum. It is also experienced as a state in which the subject professes to being filled by divinity.

It is characteristic of the subject at this time to feel that the categories of time are strained by the tensions of eternity. "Everything is touched with eternity," says one subject. "Time is no longer. Eternity has burst in," says another. "Eternity has flooded the gates of time," says still another.

The subject will experience the world as transfigured and unified. He will report himself to be caught up in an undifferentiated unity wherein the knower, the knowledge and the known are experienced as a single reality.

So striking is the correspondence between these subjects in the similar unfolding and structural patterning of their experiences that one is moved to consider the possibility of a phenomenology of the religious consciousness (at least, of that consciousness evoked in the psychedelic state). All seem to descend to an autonomous region of the psyche wherein resides the shadow of ontological constructs heretofore suggested by Jungian and depth psychologists. At the depths of the phenomenological descent resides the mystical and philosophical apprehension of Being, the subject experiencing Being as the ground and origin of all its configurations, with the difference, however, that in the psychedelic-mystic state he is freed from the interpretive prism of perception and reflection and claims a direct knowledge of Being—an experience of unfiltered primordial energy unknown to the professional ontologist. Thus, he is not likely to compound the ontologist's error of forcing Being's dynamic fecundity into the rigid framework of banal conceptualization. Rather does he conceive of Being as flux and nexus; process and concretion—autonomously derived, but substantiated in the crucible of consciousness.

The method of ontology is to posit a series of hierarchical linkages through which Being may exfoliate from transpersonal levels into consciousness. A cross-sectional observation of the total psychedelic experience reveals such an exfoliation in its various strata. For example, the level above the mysterium, the level of phylogenetic material, appears from the evidence to be composed of largely autonomous, transpersonal structures which serve to condense the primordial energy in myths and rituals, ideal forms, symbols, psychic categories—which in turn give operational momentum to conscious life and society. The unconscious phylogenetic stage, then, can feed the conscious ontogenetic layers with its wealth of evolutionary and cultural deposits, and, in so doing, help the ontogenetic to free itself from its narrow personalistic and mechanistic disposition. The floodtides of Being reach upward to consciousness and concretion and ontogenetic man extends his creative awareness to old constellations and new possibilities.*

* Grateful acknowledgment is here made to the *International Philosophical Quarterly* for permission to reproduce in these pages the article of Jean Houston, "Psycho-Chemistry and the Religious Consciousness," which appeared in the *Quarterly*, vol. 5, no. 3 (September 1965), pp. 397–413.

Selected Bibliography
for Further Reading

Arberry, A. J., *Revelation and Reason in Islam*. New York: Macmillan, 1956.

Bennett, Charles A., *A Philosophical Study of Mysticism*. New Haven: Yale University Press, 1931.

Butler, Dom Cuthbert, *Western Mysticism*. London: Constable Publishers, 1951

Dermenghem, Emile, *Muhammad and the Islamic Tradition*. New York: Harper and Brothers, 1957.

Eliade, Mircea, *The Sacred and the Profane*. New York: Harcourt, Brace, 1959.

————, *Myths, Dreams and Mysteries*. New York: Harper and Row, 1960

De Jaegher, Paul, *An Anthology of Mysticism*. London: Burns, Oates and Washbourne, Ltd., 1935.

James, William, *The Varieties of Religious Experience*. New Hyde Park: University Books, 1963.

Nicholson, D. H. S., and Lee, A. H. E., eds., *The Oxford Book of Mystical Verse*. Oxford: Clarendon Press, 1924.

Northrop, F. S. C., *The Meeting of East and West*. New York: Harper and Brothers, 1946.

Otto, Rudolf, *The Idea of the Holy*. New York: Oxford University Press, 1952.

————, *Mysticism East and West*. New York: Meridian Books (Living Age Books), 1957.

Scholem, Gershom G., *Major Trends in Jewish Mysticism*. New York: Schocken Books, 1954.

Smith, Margaret, *Readings from the Mystics of Islam*. London: Luzac and Co., Ltd., 1950.

———, *Studies in Early Mysticism in the Near and Middle East*. London: Sheldon Press, 1931.

Stace, Walter T., *The Teachings of the Mystics*. New York: Mentor Books (New American Library), 1960.

Thurston, Herbert, *The Physical Phenomena of Mysticism*. Chicago: H. Regnery Co., 1952.

Underhill, Evelyn, *The Mystic Way*. New York: E. P. Dutton and Co., 1913.

———, *Mysticism*. New York: Noonday Press, 1955.

———, *Worship*. New York: Harper and Row, 1957.

Wach, Joachim, *Types of Religious Experience Christian and non-Christian*. Chicago: University of Chicago Press, 1951.

Watts, Alan W., *The Supreme Identity*. New York: Pantheon, 1950.

Zaehner, Robert C., *Hindu and Muslim Mysticism*. London: University of London, 1960.

———, *Mysticism Sacred and Profane*. New York: Oxford University Press, 1957.

Zimmer, Heinrich, *Myths and Symbols in Indian Art and Civilization*. New York: Pantheon, 1946.

———, *Philosophies of India*. New York: Pantheon, 1951.

I. Index of Texts

205

II. General Index

Note: The texts of the mystical writings have not been indexed due to the complexities involved in any attempted cross-cultural evaluation of such specialized terminology.

Memphite theology, 114 note
ministry, 187
monism, XIII, 41, 43, 140, 151
monotheism, 114 note, 116, 116 note
mystery, 41, 42
mystical act characteristics, 13, 22
Mystical Body, 43
mystical experience, X, XI, XII, 15,
  16, 21, 27, 28, 31, 40, 41, 43, 45,
  46, 111, 141
mysticism in art, X, 5
mystical love, 15, 20, 24, 33, 41, 42,
  44, 46, 47
mystical phenomena, XI, 195ff.
mystical process, XI, 7, 8, 9, 10, 11,
  12, 22, 25, 26, 27, 31, 111, 151,
  170, 186
mystical state, 7, 9, 11, 12, 13, 15,
  21, 22, 26, 41, 42, 43, 45, 46, 140,
  151

negation, 150
negative theology, 45 note
Neo-Manichaeism, 129
nihilism, 150
Nirvana, 151
Noble Eight-fold Path, 150, 151
non-monism, 15, 43
non-rational, 9
non-theism, XIII, 150

Oneness, 7, 9, 10, 11, 14, 15, 39, 42,
  44, 46, 47
optimism, 138, 149
Osiris, 117
Other, XI, 8, 11, 26
otherness, 40

pantheism, 140
participation, 44, 46, 113, 141
passivity, 171
Persia, 129ff., 148

person, personal, 14, 16
pessimism, 138, 149, 150
political, 5
prayer, 28, 39
Presence, 7, 8, 9, 11, 12, 15, 23, 25,
  26, 40, 41, 43, 44, 46, 113, 132,
  140, 165
priesthood, 187
prophet, 12, 45, 129, 132
psyche, 46
psychological phenomena, XI, 195ff.
Ptah, 114
puritanism, 129

quietism, 172

Ra, 115, 116, 117
rapture, 32, 33
rational, 9, 10, 11, 12, 22, 23, 27,
  165
realization, 9, 10, 23, 44
rebirth, 148
reflectivity, 8, 9, 13, 27
reform, reformation, 19, 21, 116
reincarnation, 138
religion: definition, 7
religious mysticism: definition, 7
restoration, 161
resurrection, 117
revelation, 12, 37, 38, 40, 45, 117,
  182
reversal, 12, 26
Ricci, 182
ritual, 163

sacraments, 28, 33
Sacred, X, XI, 7, 9, 12
salvation, 29, 182
Saoshyant, 130
Scripture, XII, 20, 32, 37, 42, 181
secular, 138, 164, 183
self, 43, 46, 47, 140